AF324159

F·O·O·T·B·A·L·L
STARS
1985

KEVIN LAMB

CENTRAL LIBRARY
OGDENSBURG

NORTH COUNTRY LIBRARY SYSTEM
Watertown, New York

**CONTEMPORARY
BOOKS, INC.**
CHICAGO

Library of Congress Cataloging in Publication Data

Lamb, Kevin.
    Football stars, 1985.

    1. Football players—United States—Biography.
I. Title.
GV939.A1L36   1985   796.332'092'2 [B]   85-14912
ISBN 0-8092-5141-8

Photo credits:

Photo on page 5 by Robert L. Smith; on page 15 by Kurt Jupin; on pages
37 and 38 by Don Ferguson; on pages 50 and 51 by M. Fabus; on pages
68, 69, 110, and 111 by Nate Fine Photo; on page 73 by Lou Witt; on page
95 by Tom Albert; on pages 101 and 102 by Rick Kolodziej; on page 119
by Joel Zwink; and on page 120 by Sam Stone.

Copyright © 1985 by Kevin Lamb
All rights reserved
Published by Contemporary Books, Inc.
180 North Michigan Avenue, Chicago, Illinois 60601
Manufactured in the United States of America
Library of Congress Catalog Card Number: 85-14912
International Standard Book Number: 0-8092-5141-8

Published simultaneously in Canada by Beaverbooks, Ltd.
195 Allstate Parkway, Valleywood Business Park
Markham, Ontario L3R 4T8 Canada

CONTENTS

INTRODUCTION

You might be wondering why one of your favorite players didn't get into this book. It wasn't personal, honest. There is no list of the NFL's top 40 stars by proclamation. People disagree. That's why they make chocolate and vanilla, and why Baskin Robbins changes its flavors of the month. To limit the pack to 40, some deserving players had to be left out.

Fred Dean belongs, for one. I tried to shoehorn him into the lineup. But there were some ground rules, and Dean is an excellent example of how they worked against older players who rarely touch the ball and play for good teams.

First off, each team had to be represented. That's 28 players off the bat. There were only 12 at-large spots, a maximum of two extras per team. That was Todd Christensen's roadblock. San Francisco should have had the maximum, maybe, but do you take Dean or Dwight Clark or Eric Wright or Dwight Hicks or Keith Fahnhorst or Randy Cross or Keena Turner or Roger Craig? And whom do you kick off?

Then came the problem of defining a star. Stardom suggests more than simply the best players. Popularity is an element of stardom, and youth is an element of popularity, fair or not. Another element is position. It most certainly isn't fair that quarterbacks, running backs, and receivers get the bulk of football's star attention, but they do, and that's why they account for 23 of these 40.

Most of the other 17 are either standard-setters or trendsetters or budding juggernauts at their positions. But that doesn't mean that Clay Matthews, Hugh Green, E. J. Junior, Rod Martin, Jim Collins, Andre Tippett, and Mike Merriweather aren't excellent linebackers. Or that Dennis Smith, Todd Bell, Michael Downs, Vann McElroy, Louis Wright, Everson Walls, and Darrell Green aren't among the cream of the defensive backfield crop.

Linemen got particularly short shrift, especially on offense. Mike Webster, Mike Kenn, Russ Grimm, Joe Jacoby, John Ayers, Kent Hill, Dennis Harrah, Bill Bain, Jimbo Covert, Mike Munchack, Sean Farrell, and Ron Hallstrom would be some of the game's reigning and blossoming stars if football involved moving the ball so we can watch people block, instead of vice versa. There was room on defense for a full all-pro line, but Jim Burt, Joe Nash, Curtis Greer, Jacob Green, Jeff Bryant, Richard Dent, Art Still, Doug English, Dave Butz, Doug Betters, Bob Baumhower, Ed Jones, and Greg Brown have nothing to apologize for.

The older players here are strong Hall of Fame candidates, some of them shoo-ins. So are Dan Fouts, Tony Dorsett, and Earl Campbell, but they've tailed off in the last year or two. Jack Youngblood, Charlie Joiner, John Stallworth, and John Riggins were going strong last year, but their careers seem near an end. As does William Andrews's, for a more heartbreaking, but also more common, reason. He was injured. The older players I included—Jan Stenerud, Joe Theismann, John Hannah, Walter Payton, Randy White, Steve Largent, Mike Haynes, and Lee Roy Selmon—are still playing as well as they ever did.

Please have fun arguing over who should have made it, or who should be the next 20. What's the point of being a sports fan if you can't get into arguments?

But whether or not you agree with all 40 selections, it's a representative group of football stars. What, then, ties them together? What can we learn about them?

More than anything, they're still battling for their jobs whether they have to or not. Some of them have been stars since grade school, but many of them had to beat out people throughout their careers. They climbed up their depth charts and beyond because they had big enough egos to believe they were the best, yet strong enough insecurities to keep looking over their shoulders, and to underestimate their distance from the next guys behind them. They're generally smart players, and if they're not book scholars, they're still smart enough to know anything gained through hard work can be lost without it.

Not surprisingly, 24 of the 40 were first-round draft choices. Seven more were second-rounders. But even those players didn't necessarily sail smoothly to the top. Haynes, White, Kellen Winslow, Howie Long, Mark Gastineau, and Chris Hinton, to name a few, were relative nobodies as late as the year before they were drafted.

The lower choices had to prove themselves to pro coaches who had no financial incentives to be patient with them. Roy Green, Theismann, and Largent were fourth-round picks. Mark Clayton was an eighth-rounder. Dave Krieg, Deron Cherry, and Warren Moon were not drafted.

A look at the colleges represented shows an inordinate number of small-time football schools. Only 29 came from major conferences or independents. Others went to such hinterlands as Henderson State, Milton, Villanova, Portland State, and East Central Oklahoma State. The only Big Ten school represented is Northwestern. More predictably, the only colleges to produce three players are Notre Dame, Southern Cal, and Alabama.

All 40 have natural talent. Some have more than others, but you have to have a certain minimum even to be considered by an NFL team, and that minimum is a high one. As much as anything, this book shows why those talented athletes aren't wondering what might have been.

MARCUS ALLEN
IMPROVISATIONS AND EXCITATIONS

Los Angeles Raiders
Born March 26, 1960, at San Diego, California
Height, 6.02. Weight, 210.

YEAR	CLUB	G	RUSHING				PASS RECEIVING			
			ATT	YDS	AVG	TD	NO	YDS	AVG	TD
1982	Los Angeles Raiders NFL	9	160	697	4.4	11	38	401	10.6	3
1983	Los Angeles Raiders NFL	15	266	1014	3.8	9	68	590	8.7	2
1984	Los Angeles Raiders NFL	16	275	1168	4.2	13	64	758	11.8	5

PASSING						
ATT	COMP	PCT	GAIN	TD	INT	AVG
4	1	25.0	47	0	0	11.75
7	4	57.0	111	3	0	15.85
4	1	25.0	38	0	0	9.5

Marcus Allen started to his left, but all he saw was a posse of tacklers. When he spun around, he appeared to be headed for the right sideline. No, wait. There was a crack of daylight in the middle of the line. Allen was through it before the tacklers could react. The chase was on. "I really screwed up on that play," Allen said after pulling away from everyone for a 74-yard touchdown, the longest ever in a Super Bowl.

He is the Robin Williams of running backs. A script stifles him. He doesn't really have the speed or power to turn Xs and Os into first downs and touchdowns. But let him ad lib, and he steals the show. He cuts behind a block and heads for the sideline until tacklers surround him there. Then he cuts back toward the center of the field, leaving those linebackers and safeties with their arms flailing, as though they're on a capsizing boat. As O. J. Simpson says, "Marcus can look great twisting and spinning for eight yards."

"A lot of times, I don't know what the hell I'm doing out there," Allen said after that 1984 Super Bowl, when he was MVP of the Los Angeles Raiders' victory. "I kind of react and just hope things go right. I let my feet take over."

The regular season had been disappointing for Allen. He complained that he wasn't carrying the ball enough, less than 17 times a game compared to nearly 40 when he set 12 NCAA records as a Southern Cal senior. Owner Al Davis explained how the Raiders wanted to keep Allen healthy for longer than four years. That made sense, but still. He had run for 100 yards only once. His longest gain was 19 yards. Suspicion arose that he maybe had played over his head when he was Rookie of the Year in 1982.

So? Some would say he always has played over his head. Great players do that. If that was the case, he took flight once more for the playoffs, when his 466 yards in three games were nearly half his output for the 16-game warm-up act. He averaged eight yards per carry. He set Super Bowl records with 191 yards rushing and a 9.5 average. Like all great entertainers, he gave his best performance at the best time to have it.

Not that Allen has to run for 100 yards to help the Raiders. "I think he's a classic all-around back," Davis says. He blocks like the I-formation fullback he was as a USC sophomore. "He's as good a blocker as he is a runner," Raider guard Curt Marsh says. He passes like the quarterback he was in high school. He threw for three touchdowns in 1983. And catching passes may be the thing he does best. He has led AFC backs in receptions all three of his seasons, and his 11.8-yard average gain last year was almost unheard of for a back.

"I think he can become the first back in pro ball ever to rush for 1,000 yards and have 1,000 yards in pass receptions in a season," Simpson says.

"He's so good, he makes everybody around him a little better," Raider guard Mickey Marvin said when Allen was a rookie. Wide receiver Cliff Branch said Allen's presence would add three years to his career. Quarterback Jim Plunkett said he was having "more fun than ever." Allen's 116 yards rushing in his first game were the most by a Raider in five years. He was the first back in seven years to lead the league in scoring, and the first rookie in seventeen years. The Raiders climbed back to prominence from 7–9 to 8–1.

"Plus," said Marvin, "he's got that sparkle in his eye, and his manner that wins over everyone. He's just a good guy." Allen may look like a movie star, but the surest way to wipe that smile off his face is to suggest he's a hot dog. He didn't even want to play quarterback in high school because it was so important to just be one of the guys. When the Raiders nicknamed him E.T. for his long neck, he just winked and decided to tell people it stood for Extra Talented.

Allen's class off the field matches his grace between the sidelines. He plays the piano, for

When the Raiders named Allen "E. T." for his long neck, he just winked and told people it stood for "Extra Talented."

gosh sakes. "Marcus is a carbon copy of Juice," said wide receiver Bob Chandler, who played with both Allen and Simpson. "I've never seen anybody so close to O.J. I'm talking about everything—speech, mannerisms, the ease with which he deals with people, toughness, his whole approach to the game. It's uncanny. When Marcus goes in for a touchdown, he drops the ball the same way O.J. used to do it. Exactly."

He gets there pretty often, too. If he can't slither or slide past tacklers, he jumps over them, as he once did when two Atlanta Falcons awaited him at the 1-yard line after a short pass. "I had to get there one way or another," he said.

He's simply hard to tackle. "You can't drag Marcus Allen down with one arm," 49er nose tackle Manu Tuiasosopo said when he was with

Seattle. "You've got to hold him up and nail him. He just keeps coming at you."

The funny thing is, when two running backs were drafted ahead of Allen, scouts were concerned that he might be too easy to bring down with one low hit. He didn't seem very elusive, and his 40 time of 4.6 obviously wasn't very fast. Maybe he set so many records because of Southern Cal's great blockers.

The Raiders, who picked him 10th, knew better. Other scouts had forgotten to account for Allen's energy, his resolve. When he was in college, he said, "My biggest problem is I get so excited for every game that I can't stand it." His USC line coach, Hudson Houck, said, "Marcus doesn't consider life a dress rehearsal."

Allen also was new to his position. He was a full-time tailback for only two years. "Marcus taught himself how to be a great back in college," Simpson said. "He's not fast off the blocks, but he can turn that corner when other backs in the league wouldn't have turned it."

Allen's versatility nearly became a liability. Southern Cal recruited him as a defensive back out of Lincoln High in San Diego. That's what he played for four seasons, although his quarterback stats were eye-popping. For a 12–0–1 team that won the city championship, Allen threw and ran for more than 3,000 yards. He passed for 18 touchdowns, ran for 12, and returned interceptions for 4.

Southern Cal moved him to tailback on his fourth day of practice. His sophomore year at fullback was because it was Charles White's turn to win the Heisman trophy. Two years later, Allen was the fourth USC tailback in 17 years to win the Heisman.

"I didn't want to be the one who failed," he said. "So I always felt that I had to work harder than anyone else at practice."

As a senior, Allen broke the NCAA rushing record by 394 yards. He had 2,342. An *average* game was 213. He had eight 200-yard games, five in a row and eleven for his career. Those were records, too. He even led the Trojans with 34 catches. In 21 starts at tailback, Allen cleared 100 yards 20 times. And it was *he* who was grateful.

"USC really made me a football player," Allen said. "I can't quite say how much it means to me to have played there. Sometimes I sit here and wonder, why me? I mean, when I was young I dreamed about playing for USC. And then it came true. Not many guys get to have their dreams come true. But I did."

"A lot of times I don't know what I'm doing out there," Allen said after the 1984 Super Bowl. "I kind of react and just hope things go right. I let my feet take over."

GREG BELL
LONG GAINS AGAINST LONG ODDS

Buffalo Bills
Born August 1, 1962, at Columbus, Ohio
Height, 5.10. Weight, 210.

| | | | RUSHING | | | | PASS RECEIVING | | | |
YEAR	CLUB	G	ATT	YDS	AVG	TD	NO	YDS	AVG	TD
1984	Buffalo NFL	16	262	1100	4.2	7	34	277	8.1	1

The Buffalo Bills could understand the surprise. Greg Bell was certainly a gamble as the 26th choice in the 1984 draft, the first running back. "It's a little bit unusual to draft a guy Number-One and then slap his leg in a cast the next day," general manager Terry Bledsoe conceded.

The kid from Notre Dame had a bum leg. All he had to show for his last two college seasons were 61 carries and 292 yards, less than two *games'* work for Marcus Allen in college. Sure, the Bills were desperate to replace Joe Cribbs, the star halfback who had gone to the USFL defector, but Bell seemed better suited to starring on General Hospital—as a patient. His medical report was longer than his statistics: broken right leg near the ankle in the second game of his junior year, sprained right ankle in his third game as a senior, tendinitis in the ankle the rest of the season. Even Bell wasn't sure whether to bother trying football again.

"If I was the same people, I'd have asked the same questions," Bell said. The most pressing question was whether the Bills had done it again. They already could form a bucket brigade to Niagara Falls with blown first-round choices, from Walt Patulski and Phil Dokes to Perry Tuttle and Tom Cousineau, and now they had come up with a one-legged halfback who played three games a year.

Ah, but when he did play! Bell scored six touchdowns in those three senior games, including a 98-yard kickoff return and a 50-yard run. "There wasn't much film on him to review," Bledsoe said, "but we must have watched that touchdown run about 85 times. That play alone showed tremendous ability."

Bell was still big, strong, and fast. He had earned track letters as a sprinter and long jumper in the last two years. He could run 40 yards in 4.5 seconds. Besides, the Bills' doctors thought they knew why his ankle kept going south. Instead of

"I never doubt myself," Bell says. "Doubt is the last thing that's ever going to come out of my mouth."

bone connecting his lower leg and ankle bones, he had only soft tissue. The break had never fully healed. So the day after the draft, the Bills spent $2,500 on an electric impulse stimulator for his bone tissue.

The gadget worked. As a rookie, Bell didn't miss a game or a practice. His 1,100 yards rushing ranked 4th in the AFC, 13th in the NFL. And he got them for a 2–14 that rarely kept the game close enough to stick to its running game. In fact,

Bell had seven of his team's nine rushing touchdowns and 78 percent of the running backs' yards—on a two-back offense.

He took a beating. The soreness from one game would go away just in time for the next. But that was nothing. "I'd rather be sore and playing than leave games the way I used to," he said.

"All the yards you gain in college go into the history books once you leave," Bell said. "They don't mean a thing once you start running the ball in the NFL. You've got to make new yards."

That took some time. In his first 3½ pro games, Bell had 18 carries for 28 yards. Worse, his uncertain blocking assignments endangered quarterback Joe Ferguson. He lost his starting job.

But in the fourth game, against the Jets, Bell had a 49-yard second half. The next week, at Indianapolis, he ran 29 times for 144 yards. People started saying he had filled Cribbs's shoes, although Bell pointed out, "Cribbs is smaller than I am. I don't think he wears the same size." Following Cribbs was nothing compared to the pressure of staying healthy.

"I think this kid has got more power than Cribbs. "I was always using my moves," he says. a dipper and diver and juker. Greg's more overpowering."

"He can bust through a tackler," running backs coach Andy McDonald said. "He's got that burst, and a forward lean that helps him gain extra yardage. He also has a good vision and runs under control."

When Bell went to Notre Dame, he did run like Cribbs, "I was always using my moves," he says, "I'd give fakes, do 180s, I could make the air miss," Coach Dan Devine gasped at the sight, but not in awe. He said he was impressed with yards, not moves. He told Bell, "Defensive players love to tackle fakers because they're never planted. But they don't like to tackle slashers." What really sold Bell was watching an old Notre Dame-USC film and noticing O. J. Simpson, who would wear another pair of much-traveled shoes in Buffalo. "O. J. would just hit that hole and take off," Bell said, "No fakes, no moves."

That's what Bell did on the first play of the Dallas game last year, when the Bills were 0–11. He turned the corner and went 85 yards for the NFL's longest touchdown run of the season. He finished the game with 206 yards, the first 200 games against Dallas since Jim Brown did it in 1963. Buffalo's victory was the season's biggest upset.

Bell's 1,377 combined yards from scrimmage led all NFL rookies, and he made 1,282 of them in the last 12 games. He won one NFL rookie of year award, and was runner-up to Pittsburgh's Louis Lipps for the others. He played in the Pro Bowl.

The road to Honolulu was a long one, and not just figuratively. Bell made the Pro Bowl team as a last-week replacement for the Jets' Freeman McNeil. He expected to be sent to Hawaii from San Francisco, where he attended the Super Bowl, but when nobody contacted him, he went back to Buffalo late Monday night.

It was Tuesday afternoon before he arrived. Buffalo's snowstorm forced him to wait seven hours in the Rochester, New York, airport, then take a one-hour train ride. It took another two hours for Bell and some neighbors to remove the four-foot drift at his front door. Inside, he was greeted by a phone-answering machine full of congratulations. His flight to Hawaii was at 7 A.M. Wednesday. There was no time to sleep. There was also no way to reach the airport on Buffalo's officially closed streets. Only by chance did a friend drive a snow plow past his house at 6:10 A.M.

"I've taken a lot of heat over the last few years," Bell said, "and I wanted to show the people— show myself and some of the people I know best—that I can still run the ball with authority." Four feet of snow wasn't going to get in the way of accepting pro football's seal of approval.

Proving skeptics wrong was old hat by now. When Bell left Columbus, Ohio, for Notre Dame, folks back home expected him to flunk out. He earned his economics degree in 3½ years and went on to the master's program, with an eye toward law school and a career as an arbitrator after football. "I never doubt myself," Bell says. "Doubt is the last thing that's ever going to come out of my mouth."

He had been an all-state track star at South High, and his favorite sport was basketball. His team won the state championship when he was a junior. But Bell looked around. He saw a lot more NFL halfbacks under 6 feet tall than NBA guards.

When Bell was at Notre Dame, a running back coach there told him he had the ability to be a great pro back. "I said 'Thanks,' " Bell recalled. "He said, 'Don't thank me. Just do it.' "

DERON CHERRY
OPPORTUNITY'S DOORMAN

Kansas City Chiefs
Born September 12, 1959, at Riverside, New Jersey
Height, 5.11. Weight, 190.

	INTERCEPTIONS						
YEAR	CLUB	G	NO	YDS	AVG	TD	
1981	Kansas City NFL	13	1	4	4.0	0	
1982	Kansas City NFL	7	-	-	-	-	
1983	Kansas City NFL	16	7	100	14.3	0	
1984	Kansas City NFL	16	7	140	20	0	

The tryout with Kansas City would be one last fling at football. A job with Xerox was waiting. Plans for dental school were down the road. Deron Cherry wasn't kidding himself. "The chances were overwhemingly against me ever playing pro football," he says.

He was too small and too slow to play safety in the NFL, so he signed as a punter. It turned out he was even too slow for *that.* He took three steps before kicking. That was fine in college, but in the NFL, three steps give opponents enough time to draw straws for who gets to block the punt. When Cherry couldn't punt well with two steps, he might as well have gone home.

But he didn't. He *wouldn't.* "I've always been a fighter," Cherry says. "I've never been a quitter. I'd been playing football since I was nine years old. Football encompasses so much of my life, I didn't want to give it up." So he asked the coaches to give him a look at safety. One *more* last fling. He hadn't been good enough to be drafted at the position, but it was a weak spot on the Chiefs. Even when he didn't make the last cut, he was optimistic. One injury, and the Chiefs would call him back.

It happened in the season opener. In the second week of the 1981 season, Cherry was an NFL player.

Careers often begin that way. They usually stay that way. The last man on the roster is usually the first man a team tries to replace. He might hang on for two or three years, bouncing off the waiver wire a few times until he's no longer wanted.

That kind of player almost never steps into the lineup for an all-star and makes the Pro Bowl after starting one season. That's too Hollywood.

What Cherry did in 1983, intercepting seven passes and solidifying the Chiefs' secondary, couldn't have been for real.

But he did it again in 1984. Seven more interceptions, another Pro Bowl. A Xerox copy of 1983. He was telling the world it could stop rubbing its eyes now. Deron Cherry really had leaped from the fringe of the roster to the fringe of greatness.

"I've had the ability to overcome adversity, I guess," he says. "When I've had to sit back and wait my turn, I haven't just sat back and waited. I've prepared myself so that when I'm called on, I'm ready. You can be in this league for a long time and never get called on, but if you're in there and you get called on, you have to do the job."

Cherry's call came during the 1983 training camp, when free safety Gary Barbaro held out for the money he thought a three-time all-pro deserved. Cherry had moved up to nickel back in his second season, playing on passing downs, but nobody really expected him to start for the Chiefs. Defensive coordinator Bud Carson, new to the team, said, "When I first saw him, I didn't think he'd be a big part of our plans."

The pressure was on Cherry to replace the signal-caller in one of the NFL's best secondaries. This was different from the pressure we hear about year after year, the pressure of high expectations that knocks stars out of the sky. This was worse. Cherry's was the pressure of *low* expectations. "It is a challenge," he said, "but it doesn't intimidate me. It was a challenge for me to make the team the past couple of years. I'm used to that situation. It's a challenge every time you go out there."

Opponents tested him often. Free safety was obviously the weak spot in the Chiefs' secondary, so they tried to strike quickly with deep passes over the middle. Cherry surprised them. He intercepted four passes in his first five starts, six in his first eight. He led the league. He passed the test. Late in the season, teams decided he wasn't such a weak spot after all. As Cherry said, "They think maybe they can't come down the middle like they thought they could."

The other reason his interceptions slacked off was that his fingers became so swollen and tender, it hurt to tie his shoes. "Sometimes the pain's so bad they go numb for awhile," Cherry said, "but I don't think about it until after the game. If the interception's there, I'm going for it."

Barbaro had been a willing teacher, and Cherry an eager learner. It was hard to miss the similarities in their cool-headed styles. At the same time,

"You can be in this league for a long time and never get called on," says Cherry, "but if you're in there and you get called on, you have to do the job."

both could create general havoc for a defense. "I'm going to come up there and stick my nose in and hit people," Cherry said. "That gives you a lot of respect, especially in the secondary." Long passes weren't his only test.

The Chiefs' defense finished the season 10th against the pass, same as the year before. Their 10 interceptions ranked second. Through the first half of the season, when Cherry had to prove himself, they were among the top three defenses on the scoreboard.

Just because he no longer had to prove himself didn't mean he stopped trying. He still played on kicking teams like a rookie one step ahead of the cutdown ax. After the season, he sat down to review every play "to learn where I must get better." A free agent can't afford to leave his work ethic behind when he cracks the lineup.

"If there's something you want, you have to work for it," Cherry said. It means choosing priorities. At Palmyra, New Jersey High School, Cherry was a straight-A student despite the demands of football, basketball, and baseball. He turned down pro baseball contracts twice because, he said, "My main priority was to receive a degree." He went to Rutgers instead of a football factory.

Football was still important, though. He didn't like the comedown from high school quarterback to third-string sophomore free safety. Five games into his sophomore year, he was a starter. As a junior, he was Rutgers' MVP. And all along, he kept in mind what was really important and what was not.

"I think the biggest thing I've learned throughout my lifetime is, when success comes, always keep it in perspective," Cherry says. "It's here one day, but it could be gone the next." He appreciates it while he has it. He accepts public-appearance requests that other players turn down, usually for little or no money. He is aware of his responsibility as role model, "especially to young people."

One of his goodwill trips after the 1983 season took Cherry to Terry Kasperson, a quadriplegic who gave him a ceramic football player he had made. "You see his handicap and the time, effort, and energy and it's an inspiration," he said. He promised Kasperson the next ball he intercepted, which came in the 1984 opener.

For the other Chiefs, Cherry himself is ample inspiration. When he was still new to the lineup, someone asked all-pro cornerback Gary Green how Cherry was able to make so many big plays. Green's explanation was simple. He was never out of position. "I've never seen a guy study an opponent like he does," Green said.

"You try to put yourself in a position to be there and ready to make the big play," Cherry said. "So it's nice when you get the opportunity to make the interception. Any time you get the chance, you've got to take it because they don't come around too often." But then, opportunity never has had to knock twice for Cherry's reply.

Cherry intercepted four passes in his first five starts, six in his first eight to lead the league in 1983.

MARK CLAYTON
LEAPING OVER THE RAINBOW

Miami Dolphins
Born April 8, 1961, at Indianapolis, Indiana
Height, 5.09. Weight, 172.

YEAR	CLUB	G	PASS RECEIVING				PUNT RETURNS				RUSHING			
			NO	YDS	AVG	TD	NO	YDS	AVG	TD	ATT	YDS	AVG	TD
1983	Miami NFL	14	6	114	19.0	1	41	392	9.6	1	2	9	4.5	0
1984	Miami NFL	15	73	1389	19.0	18	8	79	9.9	0	3	35	11.7	0

It took a while for Mark Clayton to make people believe he's really 9 feet tall. He looks much shorter. Standing next to a tape measure, the top of his head hits the 5'9" mark. At that height, he would be handy for linemen to rest their elbows on, but an NFL wide receiver? Now, there was a tall tale.

Football isn't played in gravity boots, though. The players jump. Clayton jumps higher than most. He soars 38½ inches straight up, without a running start. When he was in college, fooling around one night with his pals, he jumped the width of a Ping-Pong table. That was too easy, he decided. So he jumped over it lengthwise.

"He changed the way I look at wide receivers," says Clayton's coach with the Miami Dolphins, Don Shula. "I was always a coach who said, 'Don't bring any of those little guys around.' I wanted tall targets, guys who are big like Cris Collins-worth and John Stallworth. If you're a little receiver in the secondary, it's tough to pick you out of a crowd. But if you're a little receiver with a 38-inch vertical jump, you become a big receiver when the ball is in the air."

That's easy to say now. Now we know Clayton led the Dolphins last year with 73 catches and a 19.0-yard average that ranked fourth in the league for receivers with at least 40 catches. We saw him catch 18 touchdown passes in his second NFL season, breaking the NFL record that had stood since 1942. He went into the last game needing two touchdowns to tie the record, and after he scored in the second quarter, Dallas safety Michael Downs said, "That's it, little man. You're shut down for the rest of the night." But Clayton scored again and broke a 14–14 tie with less than three minutes to play. And after the Cowboys came back to tie it again, Clayton broke

"He's changed the way I look at wide receivers," said Miami coach Don Shula. "I always said, 'Don't bring any of those little guys around.' But if you're a little receiver with a 38-inch vertical jump, you become a big receiver when the ball is in the air."

the record and their hearts. He caught a 63-yard touchdown pass with 51 seconds left.

He wasn't always so popular. Coaches may be willing to overlook his size now, but they used to overlook Clayton altogether. Only Indiana State and Louisville recruited him when he was an all-state tailback at Cathedral High School in Indianapolis. Even after he caught 53 passes as a senior, setting Louisville career records with 2,000 yards receiving and 20.9 per catch, he wasn't drafted until the eighth round, 223rd on the list of valued prospects. Size was a hurdle for Clayton long before it became a conversation piece.

"I'm sick of hearing about size," he said last season. "You don't play football on size. You play it on heart."

Clayton works his emotions to such a pitch that

he's often sick to his stomach before games. He sticks his chin out at adversity. Sometimes that's called exuberance, sometimes arrogance. On the final cutdown day of his rookie year, when Clayton was just another low draft choice hoping to make the AFC champions' roster, he playfully hid from the coaches behind his upturned shirt collar. "Gotta go dodge that blade," he said. When he chattered on the field in that same spirit the next season, Seattle cornerback Keith Simpson said, "He's some athlete, but sometimes his mouth runs a little faster than his feet."

Energy is Clayton's equalizer. He doesn't have the 4.3 speed of Mark Duper, the Dolphins' other 5'9" wide receiver, so he has had to work harder at his position. Where Duper can play instinctively, Clayton had to become a precise pattern runner. Where Duper could outrun doubts, Clayton had to battle them nose to nose.

"You can't back down," he says of life in the secondary. "Aggressiveness is the whole key."

The package has made him a better player than Duper, although Duper started ahead of him in the Pro Bowl. Clayton passed him in Miami's last six games, when he had 27 catches and 8 touchdowns to Duper's 13 and 1. "I think Clayton is better," said Everson Walls, Dallas Pro Bowl cornerback. "He's more physical and he'll fight you for the ball."

Dolphin quarterback Dan Marino counts on those fights. He wasn't just being modest when he dismissed the team's records for passing yards and touchdown passes by saying, "When you have great receivers like I do, it's easy to have a great day." Marino has a habit of trying to strong-arm the ball into tight coverage, and his receivers let him get away with it. "I think he realizes, after it's in the air, that he shouldn't have thrown it," Clayton says. "He just hopes we will come up with the spectacular catch. It's the confidence he has in us."

Fighting for footballs is easy after fighting for jobs. Clayton doubts he would have made the team if he hadn't agreed to return punts as a rookie. He had tried it once in his life, and he fumbled that time, but he said, "I knew I had to do a little extra to survive." His 9.6-yard average ranked 11th in the league, and he stopped worrying about being trampled after his 60-yard touchdown against the Colts.

Clayton made a splash in his sixth pro game, when he caught a touchdown pass and threw one to Duper for 48 yards. But he finished the season with six catches. He dropped some easy passes. "I just couldn't get the coaches to have confidence in me," he said. "That's what I had to change."

Working out all off-season, Clayton improved his speed from 4.6 to 4.5 and even added half an inch to his vertical jump. He planned to start in 1984. Duper had gone from no catches as a rookie to 51 in 1983, so Clayton said, "This year it's my turn. This is the season that I'll become known." Shula didn't go for the bet he proposed, that he would start if he jumped the length of a Ping-Pong table, but he relieved Clayton of the punt return drudgery.

Looking back, Shula even sees advantages to short wide receivers. The game has put emphasis on avoiding jams at the line of scrimmage, where cornerbacks take more and more advantage of their five-yard zone for legal contact. Clayton and Duper give them smaller targets. "The long striders have trouble getting away from the great athletes playing defense now," Shula says. "What you need is quickness and explosiveness getting off the line."

Durability still is a question. Teams jam Clayton with linebackers to get a size mismatch. He says defensive players "try to get their hands in your face, push you in the face mask or under your throat, and when they get you on the ground, deliver a punch to the head." He missed the end of the Pittsburgh playoff game with a shoulder injury, but he played in all but one regular-season game. Before the Super Bowl, against San Francisco's physical cornerbacks, Clayton matter-of-factly said, "My job is to catch the ball. Their job is to hit. We're going to have to bash heads and see who can survive." He doesn't back down.

"The way I see it," Clayton says, "this is a building block for the future. And in about five or six years from now I hope I'm able to walk away from the game with my health, financial security, and all the records I was shooting for. I figure if it takes any longer than that, you've got to be messing up."

ERIC DICKERSON
A STEP BEYOND THE REST

Los Angeles Rams
Born September 2, 1960, at Sealy, Texas
Height, 6.03. Weight, 218.

| YEAR | CLUB | G | RUSHING | | | | PASS RECEIVING | | | |
			ATT	YDS	AVG	TD	NO	YDS	AVG	TD
1983	Los Angeles Rams NFL	16	390	1808	4.6	18	51	404	7.9	2
1984	Los Angeles Rams NFL	16	379	2105	5.6	14	21	139	6.6	0

The jersey number was Eric Dickerson's choice. Most great running backs seem to wear 32, like Jim Brown and O. J. Simpson, or 34, like Walter Payton and Earl Campbell. No one had worn 29. That's what Dickerson liked about it. "I like to take things that nobody knows, things no one looks at, and turn it into something special. Suddenly, I see a lot of 29s. I like that a lot."

Dickerson enjoys sneaking up on people. He came to the Los Angeles Rams from relative collegiate obscurity to run for 3,913 yards in his two pro seasons. Even in his running style, he starts out slowly, almost like a lumbering tight end. He's more erect than most backs. But suddenly, he's in the open field. "He always seems to be six or seven yards downfield before any defender gets near him," says O. J. Simpson, whose single-season rushing record Dickerson broke last year. Past the pack, Dickerson shifts into overdrive. Simpson says it looks "like Captain Kirk calling Scotty, asking for warp speed."

Simpson never talked that way about other backs until Dickerson came along. He stood with Jim Brown above the other all-time rushers. He was proud of that. But Dickerson hadn't even played a full season when Simpson said, "I can't remember seeing any back with more talent and potential. And that includes myself and Gale Sayers. He's the best I've ever seen."

Dickerson has Simpson's speed at close to 230 pounds. Throw in his elusive instincts and the package is something that hasn't come together since Brown. But even Brown, who's prouder than Simpson, nudges Dickerson yet another step further.

"He's the prettiest runner in the game," Brown says. Dickerson's legs barely seem to move, let alone chop, the way other running backs propel themselves. No, Dickerson glides. Where other backs twist and spin for eight yards, Simpson says, "Dickerson will get the same yardage and make it look so damn simple."

He didn't catch many passes in college, 19 in four years. Then he caught 51 as a rookie. But he was almost as much a threat with a handoff. The Rams ran him regularly on third-and-eight.

"It's shocking how good he is," Ram coach John Robinson said.

The praise was welcome and overdue, Dickerson felt. At Southern Methodist, he grew tired of hearing about Herschel Walker, who won the Heisman Trophy Dickerson's senior year. Dickerson was sure he was at least as good as Walker, but he was frustrated by sharing time with classmate Craig James, who went to New England from the USFL last year and ran for 712 yards in the last eight games. Dickerson wasn't used to sharing the limelight. At Sealy, Texas, a town of less than 5,000 about 50 miles from Houston, he was *Parade Magazine*'s choice as the country's top high school back. He had run for 2,653 yards as a senior, including 311 and four touchdowns in the state championship game. His time in 100 yards was 9.2 seconds.

After two years at SMU, he had to be talked out of leaving by the woman he calls Mom, his great aunt Viola, who adopted him at birth because his natural mother was only 16. Dickerson wound up breaking Campbell's Southwest Conference career record with 4,550 yards rushing, despite sharing time. He tied another record with 48 touchdowns, including six runs for more than 60 yards as a senior. The Rams chose him second in the 1983 draft.

"I could tell the first day he walked in here he was something special," fullback Matt Guman said. "There was something about the way he carried himself." He didn't swagger. He knew he was good, that was clear. But he was as comfortable with his talent as other people are with freckles or bracelets. He smiled easily and his teammates found him charming.

"Some players have a way of making themselves the focal point," Robinson said. "But you have to look for Eric. He's not caught up in himself. Adulation isn't what turns him on."

Nor is the lap of luxury. Dickerson is a cheapskate and "not ashamed of it. I'm not going to spend my money on a bunch of nonsense." He didn't buy a television until nearly a year after signing for $2.2 million over four years, a figure he wanted bumped to $1 million a year after last season. He admits to one fear, "that I'd pick up the newspaper one day and read where Eric Dickerson, who had a fine eight-year career in the

O. J. Simpson says of Dickerson, "I can't remember seeing any back with more talent and potential. And that includes myself and Gale Sayers. He's the best I've ever seen." Jim Brown added, "He's the prettiest runner in the game."

NFL, was bankrupt. What I want is to pick up a newspaper one day and read where Eric Dickerson, after a fine eight-year career in the NFL, is about to open a $20 million plant."

Dickerson had the rare fortune, for a highly drafted back, to join a team with a good offensive line. He also had Robinson, a running-oriented coach, whose one-back offense was similar to SMU's I-formation. He wasn't an immediate smash. He fumbled six times in his first three games, including one in the third that set up a game-winning field goal. He was still wearing $8 shoes, and he had trouble with footing.

In his fourth game, his second carry was an 85-yard touchdown, the longest NFL run of the year. He ran for 191 and 199 in consecutive weeks. After 11 weeks, Dickerson was on a record-breaking pace. He averaged just 88 yards after that, with only one of his 20 touchdowns, but still, he set the rookie rushing record and led the Rams to the playoffs after a 2–7 season.

"I want to be consistent," Dickerson said. "My best days are the ones when I have a lot of seven, eight, ten-yard gains, not the ones when I break off a couple of long runs and have trouble with the rest."

Robinson said he learned to be more patient about picking his holes in his second season, and also to pace himself better. He had set the NFL record for carries as a rookie, and he wore out—even though he used every protective device available, scoffing at most backs' preference for minimal weight. Robinson had planned to lighten his workload last season, but when more passing led to a 5–4 start, he turned the ball over to Dickerson.

"People expect me to gain 100 yards every week," he says, "and I know when I was little and watched O.J. and he didn't gain 100 yards, I'd be disappointed. But you can't get 200 or 80 yards every time you play. You're going to have some bad days, just like a pitcher has bad days." He hasn't had many. He's 21-for-32 at breaking 100 yards, including 12 times last year for an NFL record.

In the last seven games, he averaged 165 yards. He went into the next-to-last game 212 yards behind Simpson's record, 2,003. He had never run for more than 208, but the Rams were playing Houston's league-worst defense against the run. After he flattened three or four defenders on the game-clinching touchdown run with six minutes left, Dickerson needed six yards.

His offensive teammates exhorted the defense to get the ball back. They did. Dickerson went around right end on the first play. Blockers peeked over their shoulders to catch a glimpse of history. The play went nine yards.

Dickerson graciously pointed out Simpson had set the record in just 14 games. Simpson was having none of it. "It's only a matter of time before Eric gets 2,000 yards in 14 games," he said. "The man is that good."

Dickerson gives everything he's got on the field, but at home, he's a real cheapskate and "not ashamed of it. I'm not going to spend my money on a bunch of nonsense." He didn't even buy a television until nearly a year after he signed with the Rams for $2.2 million over four years.

KENNY EASLEY
THE BALL STOPS HERE

Seattle Seahawks
Born January 15, 1959, at Chesapeake, Virginia
Height, 6.03. Weight, 206.

YEAR	CLUB	G	INTERCEPTIONS				SACKS	PUNT RETURNS			
			NO	YDS	AVG	TD		NO	YDS	AVG	TD
1981	Seattle NFL	14	3	155	51.7	1	1	-	-	-	-
1982	Seattle NFL	8	4	48	12.0	0	1	1	15	15.0	0
1983	Seattle NFL	16	7	106	15.1	0	3	1	6	6.0	0
1984	Seattle NFL	16	10	126	12.6	2	0	16	194	9.9	0

He does so many things well. He's as strong as a linebacker, but quick and fast enough to play safety. He's a sure tackler, even a devastating one. His hands are good enough to play wide receiver. But Kenny Easley does one thing that stands above everything else. "He can make plays like nobody can," Seattle coach Chuck Knox says.

Nothing is more important in Seattle's defense. The Seahawks may not smother teams like some defenses. They'll give up some first downs. They don't care. There's more than one way to take the ball from the offense, and the Seahawks figure the best way is to literally *take* it away. Then they can do something with it. They scored eight defensive touchdowns last year, two on interceptions by Easley, and doubled the total for the next best team. "The rules make it easier for the offense to make big plays," Seahawk defensive coordinator Tom Catlin says, "That's why it's more important for us to make them.

Easley is the spiritual and physical leader of the gang that led the NFL with 25 fumble recoveries and 38 interceptions—the most in the NFL since 1961—for 63 takeaways, just five short of a 23-year-old record. Their plus-24 turnover difference led the league. That's why they went 12–4 and made the playoffs.

Knox always has based his teams on ball control, but with Curt Warner injured last year, the Seahawks had the NFL's lowest rushing average per carry. The defense had to do the ball controlling. Easley led the league with 10 interceptions. He forced three fumbles and recovered one more. Seattle's defense and special teams scored

At UCLA, Easley was the team's intimidator. He shaved his head before each season. He played every game as though he had just escaped from a sealed jar after 700 years.

or set up 188 points by swiping the football, 45 percent of the team's total.

When it was time to choose the NFL's Defensive Player of the Year, Easley was a natural. He represents all that is good about the Seahawk defense. Catlin says he is "extremely aware of trying to get the football away from the other guy, constantly looking for that opportunity." That's a knack. Most players can't learn it. And it has to be instinctive. By the time a defender can think about taking the ball away, it's too late.

"I just have a lot of confidence in what I'm doing," Easley says. And a lot of athletic ability, too. Easley's strength and acceleration help make him "one of the most vicious tacklers ever," says veteran Seahawk guard Reggie McKenzie. "I mean he lathers the ball carrier." His coordination enables him to reach for the ball and without losing the positioning to make the tackle.

"It's a contagious thing," Catlin says of forcing turnovers. "One guy sees another guy do it, and he wants to get in on it, too. If you have enough guys doing it all the time, the ones who aren't picking off the ball are the exceptions instead of the one who does it."

That fevered quest for turnovers spawned an *esprit de corps* that was more reminiscent of high school teams than the pros, but absolutely essential for a team that had lost its conference rushing champion. Football teams are units, not figures on an adding machine. As Easley said, "With Curt Warner playing, we could be 2–10. It's the way the ball rolls sometimes. The only thing we deal with is reality."

Easley plays with the fury that makes him an ideal catalyst for such an up-from-nothing team. At UCLA, he was the team's intimidator. He shaved his head before each season. He was not given assignments so much as he was unleashed. He played every game as though he had just escaped from a sealed jar after 700 years.

"Playing defense suits my temperament," he says now. "It's like a release mechanism for me. Some people have to go through a ritual to get ready to play, but I don't. The game itself turns me on."

Special teams are part of it. Most players consider kicking plays drudgery, but they count, don't they? In fact, they have more yards at stake

Easley not only plays on special teams, he also volunteered to return punts. Said coach Chuck Knox, "I'd have to think a long time before I could come up with the name of another starter who ever volunteered to run back punts."

than the plays from scrimmage. Easley not only plays on special teams, he volunteered to return punts after the regular return man was injured in the fourth game. His 12.1-yard average was fourth best in the league. His 16 returns didn't qualify for the rankings, but the point is, he was only too happy to fill in at the most dangerous job on the field. "I'd have to think a long time before I could come up with the name of another starter who ever volunteered to run back punts," said Knox, who was in his 23rd NFL season.

That's not what people were saying when Easley held out during the 1984 training camp. He wanted to match Ronnie Lott's $577,000 salary, the highest for an NFL defensive back. Easley made half that. When he returned to the team without a new contract, he said, "I know I won't be here next year." His teammates wouldn't mind, people whispered. He was too selfish.

Easley has endured comparisons with Lott since their college days, when both played rover positions. Easley was a three-time consensus all-America, the first Pac-10 player to make all-conference four straight years, a UCLA record setter with 19 interceptions. But Lott played across town for Southern Cal, under the national limelight of Trojan glory. Easley was the fourth pick in the 1981 draft, four players ahead of Lott, but he didn't even approach Lott's immediate impact. His team didn't go from 6–0 to Super Bowl champion in one year.

Easley made the all-rookie teams. The Players Association voted him defensive Rookie of the Year in the AFC. He finished the season with two interceptions against Cleveland and returned one 82 yards for a touchdown. He didn't exactly spend his first season making adhesive-tape sculpture.

Since then, he has led the Seahawks in interceptions all three years and made all three Pro Bowls, becoming the first defensive all-star ever from Seattle. He was all-pro in 1983 and 1984.

He is considered a strong safety, which is usually how it works out, but Easley has stayed on the left side in every year except 1983. He is versatile enough to play free safety when the offense puts its tight end on the other side, so the Seahawks don't have to scurry around before the snap to match the offensive team's men in motion. They can concentrate on making plays.

There isn't a better prototype for strong safety. The position is the defensive complement to tight end, the one demanding the best athletic blend of speed and strength, and Easley was athletic enough to turn down basketball scholarships from Big Ten and Atlantic Coast Conference schools. He played junior varsity basketball at UCLA, which has a fair tradition in hoops. Scouts compared him with Marques Johnson. The Chicago Bulls picked him in the last round of the NBA draft. When he played quarterback at Oscar Smith High School in Chesapeake, Virginia, he was the first player in the state to gain 1,000 yards both running and passing in one season.

The Seahawks' defensive backfield coach, Ralph Hawkins, coached Ken Houston for seven years. Houston is widely considered the best strong safety ever, and Hawkins says Easley is better in some ways. As for now, Hawkins says, Easley is "the best strong safety in football."

JOHN ELWAY
THE PHENOM STRIKES BACK

Denver Broncos
Born June 28, 1960, at Port Angeles, Washington
Height, 6.04. Weight, 202.

YEAR	CLUB	G	ATT	CMP	PASSING		TD	INT	AVG	ATT	RUSHING		TD
					PCT	GAIN					YDS	AVG	
1983	Denver NFL	11	259	123	47.5	1663	7	14	6.42	28	146	5.2	1
1984	Denver NFL	15	380	214	56.3	2598	18	15	6.84	56	237	4.2	1

Denver papers assigned two reporters to the Broncos' 1983 training camp. One covered the team, one covered John Elway. People wanted to know everything from the breakfast menu to the bedtime reading of this demigod who had chosen to be the next Joe Namath instead of the next Mickey Mantle. He was the first pick of the draft, the highest-paid NFL player at $5 million for five years, and he was Denver's own salvation. The Broncos had sold out for 13 straight seasons, but their offenses had generated less than 20 points a game and a paltry 172 yards passing. As Bronco guard Tom Glassic said, "The fans think he can walk on water."

By the end of the season, more than a few of them wouldn't have thrown Elway a life ring. He was clearly in over his head when coach Dan Reeves named him the starter in training camp. He had to run one of the NFL's most intricate offenses. He didn't start and finish a victory until the team's 14th game. In the meantime, Elway lost his job to Steve DeBerg, got it back when DeBerg was injured, had a sideline shouting match with Reeves, and once even lined up behind a guard. He ranked 30th among 31 NFL quarterbacks, completed 47.5 percent of his passes, and threw 14 interceptions and 7 touchdowns.

"I really don't think it can get any worse," Elway said, looking ahead to 1984. It got much better. Elway still had more promise than production, but the promise no longer was broken. The Broncos had a 13-3 record, 12-2 in Elway's starts. He threw five touchdown passes against Minnesota. A typical game was the season-ender at Seattle, the 31–14 victory that gave Denver its first AFC West championship since 1978. Elway completed less than half his passes, but he made winning plays with his arm and his legs. "You can cover all his receivers, but you can't cover him," Seattle linebacker Keith Butler said.

One of Denver's changes in 1984 was to let Elway roll out more. He had the arm strength to throw across the field. One time at Stanford, he scrambled from his own 40 long enough for receiver Ken Margerum and Southern Cal safety Ronnie Lott to argue over whether Elway could reach the goal line. Margerum won. Elway threw a 65-yard line drive, across the field and off the wrong foot. Defenders had to respect his arm by staying downfield, which gave Elway more room to run for first downs.

But the biggest difference in Elway's second season, said Reeves, was "He was able to see things so much better." For example, he was sacked less often in half again as many attempts. As Elway's confidence soared, Reeves said, "The team gained confidence in his ability to win." He threw for more touchdowns than interceptions, completed 56.3 percent, and climbed to 17th in the quarterback rankings.

Elway had been carefully groomed to play quarterback by his father, Jack, who became Stanford's head coach after John left. When Jack took the coaching job at Cal State–Northridge near Los Angeles, he shopped for John's high school football coach before he shopped for a house. At Granada Hills, he found Jack Neumier, who sent Elway to college with an education in reading defenses.

Elway became the Pacific 10's first sophomore Player of the Year, the first sophomore all-American in 18 years. He left Stanford with 77 touchdown passes, 39 interceptions, and a 62.1 completion percentage. But he had started for teams that went 15-18 with no bowl appearances. In 1982, Stanford lost two of the three games when Elway threw for three go-ahead touchdowns after two-minute warnings. Sour medicine for a quarterback who lost so grudgingly, he and his father would play Ping-Pong all night because neither could quit after a loss.

He was certain to be the first draft choice, but by whom? Would the Colts trade that pick to the Chargers, Patriots, Rams, or Raiders, all bidding eagerly? And would Elway even play pro football?

He was a lefthanded power-hitting outfielder, excellent defensively and fast on the bases. Yankee owner George Steinbrenner was prepared to outbid any NFL team. He already had paid Elway $150,000 for six weeks of Class A ball, where he hit .318 the previous season. Baseball would delay Elway's stardom for years of minor league bus

Yankee owner George Steinbrenner was prepared to outbid any NFL team for Elway's arm. He had already paid Elway $150,000 for six weeks of Class A ball, where he hit .318.

trips, learning to hit curveballs, but he insisted he would be happy either way. "I love to take two steps into a fly ball and then hum it home, just let it fly, and watch it move," he said. "There's no feeling like that. But then, throwing a football is a much harder thing to do."

When the Colts drafted Elway, the baseball threat became real. He didn't want to play for coach Frank Kush. He wanted to play in warm weather. Fans called him a crybaby for demanding a trade, but baseball gave him leverage few draft picks had known. As he put it, "If you're a stockbroker and you can either work in New York City or Billings, Montana, you'd be mad if they made you go to Billings." The Colts sent him to Denver.

"I've never seen a young guy come in and take over a huddle the way he does," veteran Bronco receiver Steve Watson said after Elway's first few practices. "He's not afraid to get on you if he thinks you're doing something wrong. And he can do just about anything with the ball."

He released it with a quick flick from his ear,

just like Namath. In Elway's hand, footballs were darts. "He throws 50-yard bombs like 10-yard curls," Bronco cornerback Louis Wright said.

The first month of training camp, Elway did 100 interviews. The attention was no novelty. Autograph seekers had followed him in swarms through Stanford. But he never did get used to it. His twin sister, Jana, said the happiest she had seen John was at a Halloween party, where nobody recognized him behind his mask. "I'm an ordinary guy," he kept saying. "I'm not perfect."

That became all too clear in his rookie year. The worse it got, the worse it got. "The more I heard and the more I read about not playing well, the harder I tried and the more mistakes I made," he said. "The real pressure came from within. I got frustrated. I realized I couldn't think about that anymore."

Finally, in that 14th game, Elway passed for two touchdowns in Denver's 27–6 victory. "This was the game I've been waiting for," he said. "I was having fun." The next week, Denver clinched the playoffs—one year after a 2-7 season—when Elway beat the Colts with three touchdown passes in the fourth quarter. The Bronco offense no longer confused him. And when DeBerg was traded after the season, Elway said he no longer had to wonder if half his teammates thought someone else should be playing.

"The only reason I'm a celebrity," he said after one season, "is because I'm a quarterback and I was the first pick in the NFL draft. It's not because I've proven anything to anybody. That's where it's hard for me. If a kid comes up to me and asks for an autograph, I want to feel good about writing my name down on that piece of paper. I don't want to give an autograph on the basis of what I'm supposed to be able to do in the future." In his second season, that future started arriving.

"I've never seen a young guy come in and take over a huddle the way he does," says receiver Steve Watson. "He's not afraid to get on you if he thinks you're doing something wrong."

MARK GASTINEAU
SACKS APPEAL

New York Jets
Born November 20, 1956, at Ardmore, Oklahoma
Height, 6.05. Weight, 265.

YEAR	CLUB	G	SACKS
1979	NY Jets NFL	16	2
1980	NY Jets NFL	16	11½
1981	NY Jets NFL	16	20
1982	NY Jets NFL	9	6½
1983	NY Jets NFL	16	19
1984	NY Jets NFL	16	20

People assume it's theatrics. The NFL owners obviously did, when they passed the rule to outlaw Mark Gastineau's sack dance. They said any future expressions of exuberance had to be spontaneous. But Gastineau is nothing if not spontaneous.

He wasn't staging those crazy gigs just for packed stadiums and television cameras. He'll go into the same kind of dance on the Arizona desert, with no one watching but snakes and salamanders. That's where he digs on an ancient burial site for the Indian relics he collects. When Gastineau finds an especially rare piece of stoneware or jewelry, there he goes, leaping around like his pants leg is on fire.

He may have imposed his own Gastineau Rule if he had thought about the acrimony his dancing might rain down on him. He doesn't think that way, though. If it feels good, do it. Sacks make him feel like celebrating. "I've never choreographed any of it," he says. "It comes from total joy and excitement. When I make a quarterback sack, it's an emotional high. It's a feeling I can't explain. I'd like to let everybody feel that way."

Other things that feel good to Gastineau are driving a $156,000 Rolls-Royce, wearing a fur coat and one gold earring, training with Gerry Cooney, dining with Sylvester Stallone, hanging out at Studio 54, assembling a bodybuilding book, and selling a poster that features his shaved and muscular chest. He doesn't do those things because he likes a glitzy image. If he has to have an image, he'd rather it be that of a good football player who loves his family.

But hey, baby, that's a *Cleveland* image. Gastineau plays in New York. He's supposed to be *proud* he has overcome his proletarian status as a lineman to make himself the most marketable Jets player since Joe Namath. Professional sports is more in the mythmaking business than ever now that marketing experts have donated themselves to the world. Gastineau's four Pro Bowls, his NFL lead in sacks the last two years, the Players Association's 1984 award for Defensive Player of the Year—those aren't just accomplishments. They're marketing tools.

His salary is, too. Big money used to be a reward. The stars made the money. But these days, the money makes the stars. And Gastineau's star rests high atop $4 million for five years. After he signed last year, every defensive lineman whose prestige ranked with Gastineau was compelled to hold out for Gastineau money. Once again, he was the trendsetter.

And the NFL played right into the mythmakers' hands. The players and owners wagged their fingers at Gastineau for daring to have a higher profile than an anthill, and they turned him into the biggest antihero this side of professional wrestling. What a gimmick!

Gastineau is not entirely an unwilling victim of his neatly packaged image. He probably couldn't have paid for that Rolls-Royce by walking straight back to huddles in Cleveland. But he didn't set out to land in a fishbowl with half the world throwing rocks at him, either. "I'm a pretty good guy," he protests. "Everybody wants to be liked."

It's missing the point to say Gastineau is either a showboat or a showman. He treads the fine line between exuberant and obnoxious, just like millions of men who ride in commuter trains and can hardly find their chests, much less shave them. The difference is that Gastineau plays a children's game, where childlike effervescence and self-confidence are assets. Without them, he may never have played in the NFL.

Gastineau was the first player ever drafted from East Central State, an NAIA school in Ada, Oklahoma. Before he went there, his achievements never matched his size. "He wasn't aggressive," said his father, Ernie, a former pro boxer. But when the Jets drafted him in 1979, personnel director Mike Hickey boasted on "his rare competitive nature. You just could not get him to quit."

Somewhere in there, Gastineau burst out of his shell. He always had been energetic away from the football field. His archaeological passion be-

"Going up against Gastineau," says Marvin Powell, the Jets' all-pro tackle, "is like going up against the Indy 500. He accelerates with speed and finesse. He can shake and bake you and leave you standing there. He can do anything he wants."

gan in grade school, growing up in Springerville, Arizona, a small town near the New Mexico border. At 12, he took up steer roping and eventually won some money in rodeos, along with his father. "Dad always challenged me in something." Gastineau says. "An arm wrestling match, a footrace, it didn't matter."

Gastineau's football development remained arrested through one-year stints at Eastern Arizona Junior College and Arizona State. He went to East Central even though "I knew my pro ambitions were probably down the drain." But that's where he started dancing. He also took note of his exceptional 4.8 speed. So he stopped partying and started sprinting by streetlight. "If your strength is speed, get faster," he said. "To get drafted, I needed some quality that nobody else had."

Still, Gastineau probably was an eighth-round draft choice before he replaced an injured player on the Senior Bowl roster. There, in front of every NFL team's scouts, he opened eyes in practice drills and was star of the game. The Jets drafted him in the second round. They had a defensive end fast enough to run a 4.55 forty—faster than some wide receivers—and strong enough to rip a face mask right off a helmet, breaking the screws.

If there's anything Gastineau takes pride in, it's the results of his bodybuilding workouts, which he supplements with nutritional concoctions of vitamins and various animal organs. He says he shaves his chest because "I've been gifted with a great body. I want people to be able to see all of it." And people mistook his generosity for vanity.

They took his sack dance the wrong way, too. Opponents made the reasonable argument that if offensive linemen danced every time they protected the passer, the field would turn into a disco. But even Gastineau's teammates took exception. "We don't do that sort of thing," they told him. When Ram offensive tackle Jackie Slater objected to Gastineau's dance in 1983 by clobbering him from behind, he touched off a bench-clearing brawl and received thanks from linemen all over the league. Players and coaches banished him to the Pro Bowl's second team even though

that was the first year he led the league in sacks and played the run respectably.

There never had been a question about his pass rushing. In 1980, he had the most sacks by a Jet in 10 years. In 1981, he ranked second in the NFL to teammate Joe Klecko. The Jets' newly christened New York Sack Exchange led the league with 66, one short of the record, and the team improved from 4–12 to 10–5–1.

When it slipped to 7–9 the last two years after two playoff seasons, Gastineau drew two or three blockers two-thirds of the time. But his sack output remained steady. "We called all our protection schemes for Gastineau," Kansas City quarterback Bill Kenney said. "Everything. He's the best defensive end in football."

"Going against Gastineau," says Marvin Powell, the Jets' all-pro tackle, "is like going up against the Indy 500 speed race. He doesn't just move. He accelerates with speed and finesse. He can shake and bake you and leave you standing there. He can run over you. He can do anything he wants."

In objecting to Gastineau's famous sack dance, opponents made the reasonable argument that if offensive linemen danced every time they protected their quarterback, the field would look like a disco.

ROY GREEN
OPEN ALL DAY

St. Louis Cardinals
Born June 30, 1957, at Magnolia, Arkansas
Height, 6.00. Weight, 195.

YEAR	CLUB	G	PASS RECEIVING				PUNT RETURNS				KICKOFF RET.			
			NO	YDS	AVG	TD	NO	YDS	AVG	TD	NO	YDS	AVG	TD
1979	St. Louis NFL	16	1	15	15.0	0	8	42	5.3	0	41	1005	24.5	1
1980	St. Louis NFL	15	-	-	-	-	16	168	10.5	1	32	745	23.3	0
1981	St. Louis NFL	16	33	708	21.5	4	-	-	-	-	8	135	16.9	0
1982	St. Louis NFL	9	32	453	14.2	3	3	20	6.7	0	-	-	-	-
1983	St. Louis NFL	16	78	1227	15.7	14	-	-	-	-	1	14	14.0	0
1984	St. Louis NFL	16	78	1555	19.9	12	-	-	-	-	1	18	18.0	0

In their second 1981 game, the St. Louis Cardinals were so short of wide receivers, they put their back-up strong safety in for one play. Coach Jim Hanifan told him to just run fast down the sideline. Nobody expected quarterback Neil Lomax to actually throw him the ball. But there it went. The safety, Roy Green, wrestled the ball away from cornerback Everson Walls, Dallas's rookie who would lead the league in interceptions. He gained 60 yards to the Cowboy 1. Hanifan decided to let Green have some more plays on offense, and a career was born.

The next week Green started at wideout, but he still played defense. He became the first player since 1957 to intercept and catch a pass in the same game. His four catches for 115 yards included a 58-yard touchdown. Afterward, Hanifan told Green, "Even in my dreams, you didn't look that good." Green, barely breathing hard, talked about taking his wife out dancing.

Four years later, Green is still playing wide receiver and still looking terrific. He has caught passes in 56 straight games, every game he has played on offense. For 1983 and 1984, his 156 catches are the most by any NFL wide receiver, and his 26 touchdowns and 2,782 yards lead all receivers. He shared the NFC lead with 78 catches in 1983 and led the NFL with 1,555 receiving yards in 1984. There are people who call him the best wide receiver in football.

But for sheer amazement, Green will never match his 1981 season. Besides starting at wide receiver, a position he hadn't played since high school, Green was the nickel back on defense and played on all four kick coverage and return teams. "The only thing Roy hasn't done is tape our ankles," tackle Dan Dierdorf said. He played 45 minutes a game, as many as 108 plays.

"When I was a senior in high school, I never left the field," Green said. "Your body gets used to it."

His body, maybe. "He's totally amazing," Hanifan said. "He never gets tired. I'd like to see what he could do in a marathon run."

Hanifan had toyed with putting Green on offense earlier that season, when he watched him fool around with some teammates after practice. They were throwing the ball around, and Green was making sharp cuts and sure-handed catches. He also knew the offensive plays. He had made it a point to listen in at quarterbacks' and receivers' meetings. "I wanted to know what they were thinking when they tried to get open," he said.

What makes Green special is his knack for getting open, a skill most receivers need years and years to develop. It seems like a simple thing, getting open. Fans don't appreciate it when they see an easy coach and mutter, "He was so wide open, *I* could have caught that one." The hard part is getting that wide open. Good athletes are paid to keep it from happening.

"People talk about his speed and his great hands," Lomax says, "but I look more at his intelligence and his cool and confidence. He has great ability to adjust to any type of coverage." A former Cardinal told his new teammates last year that the Cards base their offense on the assumption he can get open against any defense. Jimmy (The Greek) Snyder calls him Diner because "He's open all the time."

St. Louis fans call him Jet Stream because he can run 40 yards in 4.3 seconds. He jokes with Lomax that the quarterback should figure out the longest pass that's possible to catch, then put a little extra on it. "His acceleration is very exciting to see," Lomax says, "When he goes down 40 or 50 yards and the ball is overthrown by 10 yards, he puts that thing in turbo and goes for it. I've never seen anybody like that."

"I've always been able to find an extra burst when I need it," Green says, "When I'm running side by side with a defensive player, he's beaten."

If he can't run away from the defender, Green fights the ball away from him. He attacks it like a defensive back, which, of course, he used to be. "There are certain guys you want to throw to, guys you know will hang on to the ball," said Jim

St. Louis fans call him "Jet Stream" because he runs the 40 in 4.3 seconds. Jimmy the Greek calls him "Diner" because he's always open.

Hart, Green's quarterback for much of 1981, "Roy's one of those."

He isn't nasty about it. Green is very seldom nasty about anything. Even his game face is a smile, which has drawn some disconcerted double-takes from new teammates. "I'm pretty loose at all times," he says. And why not? Football players may put on battle armor, but they're playing a children's game. As Hanifan says, "The thing about Roy is, football is fun for him. He really enjoys playing."

That wasn't always so. When Green went out for the eighth grade team in Magnolia, Arkansas, his football career nearly ended before it began. He was one of the biggest players, so the coach put him on the offensive line. Green went home. He didn't return to the sport until he was a high school junior. The next year, he played all the non-line positions on offense and defense, and he kicked off.

Still, his favorite sport was baseball. He kept playing center field through his first NFL off-season, when he batted near .500 for the semipro Magnolia Raiders. He also played for the state high school basketball champs and sprinted for the college track team at Henderson State, in Arkadelphia, Arkansas.

Henderson State's coach, Sporty Carpenter, had some fool notion that football players should stick to either offense or defense. Green was a cornerback. He used to beg Carpenter to let him play offense, but the coach was resolute until the game against Arkansas-Monticello, when Green returned a kickoff and two interceptions for touchdowns. Green wound up playing a handful of offensive downs in college, and once he threw a 60-yard touchdown pass as a halfback.

He was an NAIA All-American for a team that won two conference championships, but the conference was the Arkansas Intercollegiate, not the Big Eight. Green wasn't drafted until the fourth round in 1979. After missing most of training camp with an injury, he was afraid he wouldn't make the team. But his 106-yard kickoff return as a rookie still shares the NFL record. In later years, he also scored on a punt return and a run from punt formation. He never scored on an NFL interception, but he did sack one quarterback in 1980.

Hanifan ended Green's two-platoon days in 1982, for the understandable reason that he was too good a wide receiver to waste time elsewhere. The strike slowed his progress in 1982, but he caught the Cardinal's playoff-clinching touchdown of eight yards with 27 seconds left against the Giants. It was his third winning catch in a final minute. In 1983, the NFL Alumni named him Wide Receiver of the Year. In 1984, he had six 100-yard game times and scored two touchdowns in four, including the upset of Dallas and the second-half comeback at Washington that nearly put the Cards in the playoffs. His 19.9-yard average gain led all receivers with more than 35 catches.

"When I see the ball coming," Green says, "I always say, touchdown. I think that helps me concentrate more. I'm usually relaxed when I'm catching. You know what you've done in practice. Why put more pressure on yourself just because it's a game?"

Talk about versatility: in 1981, Green started at wide receiver, was the nickel back on defense, and played on all four kick coverage and return teams. "The only thing Roy hasn't done for us is tape our ankles," tackle Dan Dierdorf said.

DAN HAMPTON
A WILD AND CRAZY TERROR

Chicago Bears
Born September 19, 1957, at Oklahoma City, Oklahoma
Height, 6.05. Weight, 270.

YEAR	CLUB	G	SACKS
1979	Chicago NFL	16	4½
1980	Chicago NFL	16	11½
1981	Chicago NFL	16	9
1982	Chicago NFL	9	7
1983	Chicago NFL	11	5
1984	Chicago NFL	15	11½

Dan Hampton couldn't understand all the fuss, just because he was going to play football in five days. "It's been eighteen days since I was on the operating table," he said. So he went out and made two sacks for the Chicago Bears barely three weeks after arthroscopic knee surgery. "He's a little different from most people when it comes to pain," Bear coach Mike Ditka says.

It's not that, Hampton insists. Other guys play with pain, too. He's not so much valiantly brave as he is childishly enthusiastic. "You only get 16 days a year to play," he says. "After all that working and running and lifting in the off-season, you don't want to miss any. All of us on the defensive line have a great desire to get to the quarterback. There's no way you can do it sitting on the bench. More than anything else, I just don't want to be left out in the rush."

He's usually not. Hampton probably is the NFL's best inside pass rusher. He led all defensive tackles in sacks in 1982 and ranked third in 1984, sloughing off in 1983 because of the knee surgery. He won some Defensive Player of the Year awards for both his healthy seasons and made the Pro Bowl, as he had done in 1980 as a defensive end.

The move inside didn't thrill him. Hampton's long legs go almost up to his elbows, and he knew how blockers can't resist banging their helmets against defensive tackles' knees. Pain is one thing. A career-ending injury is different. Besides, most sack leaders launch themselves from the outside, where the traffic is thinner. Hampton remembers his sacks the way a pro golfer can recite his round stroke by stroke. "It's so hard to get a sack anymore, they're all precious," he says. He was reluctant to make them more precious by stepping into the teeth of double-team blocking.

But the Bears weren't moving Hampton inside to put a cap on his pass rush. He was replacing Alan Page, probably the best inside pass rusher ever, and Hampton was the only one who could fill his starting blocks. Defensive coordinator Buddy Ryan believes, almost uniquely, that the most important pass rushers are the tackles, not the ends. Tackles are the ones who can block a quarterback's view downfield. He also wants Hampton making plays on both sides of the field.

In the Bears' five-lineman "46" defense, Ryan frees Hampton from double-team blocking by putting him over the center and teammates over each guard. "When Dan Hampton gets on a center and the center doesn't have immediate help, then the center's got problems," Cowboy coach Tom Landry says. Bear center Jay Hilgenberg, who practices against Hampton, says, "By the time you finish your snap, especially in the shotgun, his arm's around your shoulder. It's pretty hard to get back and pass block that way. His arms are so long and quick and strong. He gets you leaning one way, you're off-balance, and then he comes back at you with that club from the other side."

Although his 11½ sacks ranked second on the team last year, Hampton was the biggest reason the Bears set an NFL record with 72. The Los Angeles Rams know that. They played the Bears in the only game Hampton missed, with a torn bicep muscle, and it also was the only time the Bears didn't get a sack. Ram offensive line coach Hudson Houck visited the press room each day that week to find out the latest on Hampton. "We're not just talking about some good player," offensive coordinator Jimmy Raye said. "We're talking about a guy who can be a stud with even one arm." When Ram guard Kent Hill talked to a reporter for a story on Randy White as the NFL's best defensive lineman, he couldn't stop talking about Hampton.

Hampton was embarrassed just appearing on the injury report, of which he says, "All that questionable-probable stuff is a bunch of crap. They'd be a lot closer to the truth if they made the categories 'sissy,' 'punking out,' and 'squirreling out.' There's no other way you can think in football. Everybody's got to be doing his day's work." He started the first 65 games in his career

Hampton remembers his sacks the way a pro golfer can recite his round, stroke by stroke.

before his knee operation, which turned out to be the first of three, after his other knee had been cut twice. When his back kept going into spasms in 1980, he dismissed the problem as "just some vertebrae rolling out of alignment."

To understand Hampton's relationship with pain, it helps to realize that he spent six months in a wheelchair when he was 11. His brother was shooting a BB gun at him, so he climbed a tree. He was 40 feet from the ground when he fell. He broke both legs and an arm. Telling the story, he couldn't stop laughing. After flying to Chicago from Fayetteville, Arkansas, he said, "You don't buy tickets to fly out of there, you buy chances." This is a man who decided once to pick up a five-foot alligator, just for the heck of it.

"I'm not what a lot of people would call mean," Hampton says. "We had players in college that were mean. They threw cats at moving cars, things like that. But I've got a temper, and a lot of times it flares up on the field. It's not something I have to conjure up. After one season, our coach told me we had nine personal fouls that year and I had all nine."

He bloomed late as a football player. His first sport at Jacksonville High near his farm home in

Cabot, Arkansas, was the marching band. He was the biggest saxophone player, so the football coach talked him into trying out. Even in college, before his senior season, a national magazine wrote a story picking Arkansas as national champion and didn't mention Hampton. He wasn't invited to any all-star games after the season.

The Bears' 40 time on him was 5.15 before scout Jim Parmer visited the school a few weeks before the draft. "He came bounding into the room like an overgrown pup," Parmer said, and asked if he could run another 40. "Usually, you have to track guys down and beg them to run for you." Hampton said he hadn't been able to warm up before his 5.15. This time, he ran a 4.85. Speed was all he'd been lacking. But he still thought some friend was playing a joke when the Bears called to say they just picked him fourth in the 1979 draft.

Even now, Hampton doesn't consider himself an exceptional athlete. "I just take the attitude, this is the line of scrimmage, and you're not getting by," he says. "If you get 11 men who are committed to that, and they're fanatic about it, crazy men, you can stop a lot of people just on sheer effort."

"Watching him from behind on a running play, he looks like a big shark going after some fish," Bear linebacker Al Harris says. "You see a blocker and the guy with the ball, and then Dan gets in there and you don't see them anymore. He creates a lot of havoc."

He takes unusual pride in his run defense, but the play he likes best is "blind-siding the quarterback. It's better when he doesn't know you're coming. That's how I excite myself." That's all. No celebration. No dance. No high fives. He doesn't even feel a tingly rush, he says. "You don't have time. You're expected to make sacks. And you've got to line up and try to do it on the next play."

"I'm not what a lot of people would call mean," Hampton says. "We had players in college that threw cats at moving cars. They were mean. But I've got a temper, and a lot of times it flares up on the field. One season, my team had nine personal fouls and I had all nine."

JOHN HANNAH
MAYBE THE BEST EVER

New England Patriots
Born April 4, 1951, at Canton, Georgia
Height, 6.03. Weight, 265.

YEAR	CLUB	G
1973	New England NFL	13
1974	New England NFL	14
1975	New England NFL	14
1976	New England NFL	14
1977	New England NFL	11
1978	New England NFL	16
1979	New England NFL	16
1980	New England NFL	16
1981	New England NFL	16
1982	New England NFL	8
1983	New England NFL	16
1984	New England NFL	15

The first thing people notice about John Hannah is his power. Blocking straight ahead, he can drive a defensive lineman five yards downfield. He has taken safeties as far as 20 yards.

The power comes from muscular 33-inch thighs that look like they could support a bridge. They're his most prominent feature, aside from the baby-faced smile that has endured 34 years. They're the reason Hannah's teammates called him Hamhocks when he played at Alabama, then simply Hog in his 12 seasons with the New England Patriots.

But they're not the reason a throng of admirers calls Hannah the best offensive lineman ever to play pro football. There's little doubt he's the most overpowering guard. The question to debate is which of his more subtle skills sets him farthest ahead of the merely great linemen.

His agility? The most important thing NFL linemen do is protect the passer, and strength isn't enough for that. It takes quick feet, too. The blocker has to dance with the pass rusher, anticipate his moves, and keep him chest to chest. Hannah's agility goes beyond just pass blocking, though. He's also quick from side to side. The man he's blocking can sneak around the end, but Hannah follows him all the way, quick step for quick step, in a ground-shaking ballet. "Once in a while he does things that are unbelievable," former Patriot coach Ron Erhardt said.

Hannah's balance is no less remarkable. He stays on his feet. That not only makes him an imposing obstacle in any tackler's way, it makes him mayhem on the move. After blocking his man, he can continue downfield, leveling more would-be tacklers.

He's fast, too. His 4.8 time for 40 yards is tight end speed. Jim Ringo, the Patriot line coach who played for Green Bay, says, "John has better pulling speed than Fuzzy Thurston and Jerry Kramer, although he's 20 pounds heavier than both."

He is an excellent athlete who happens to be enormous. As a wrestler, he won the National Prep Championship and was unbeaten his freshman year at Alabama. Then he switched to track, which wouldn't take him away from spring football practice, and set Crimson Tide records in the shot put and discus.

But for all the eye-popping things Hannah does with his 265-pound frame, the best thing about him may be his frame of mind. His aggressive attitude is more common in defensive linemen. He doesn't absorb blows, he gives them. And he has just enough insecurity to keep him on a tireless quest for ways to improve.

"John has more intensity than other guys at the Pro Bowl," says Joe DeLamielleure, another perennial all-pro guard. "He works hard. If you take a guy with that much talent and he works like a guy who has no talent, then he becomes super."

Hannah has been all-pro the last nine years. He made the Pro Bowl every year since 1976, too, except for 1977, when voting coaches punished him for his contract holdout three games into the season. That didn't keep the Players Association from electing him the league's Most Valuable Offensive Lineman from 1977 through 1980, the first four years the award was given.

But still, he goes into every game with a real fear. It's not the fear of injury, he says, "but the fear of being humiliated, being made to look bad." It's the kind of pride that keeps the best players from accepting compliments.

Even when he was young, Hannah would ask his father to critique his play. "I always tried to be honest. If he played bad, I told him," Herb Hannah says. That's what young John wanted. The old man had played for the Giants in the early 1950s. He knew what to look for in a lineman.

Although Bear Bryant may not have taught Hannah how to pass block, "he did teach us what it took to win, and what it meant to win."

"I learned from him," Hannah says. "We talked a lot after games. It brought us closer together. He kept me going, hustling, enjoying the game. A lot of fathers live their dream through their kids. They put pressure on them, try to be Junior Bear Bryants, and turn them away eventually. All my dad said was, 'Son, if you're going to do it, I think you ought to give it all you've got.' He didn't make me play. He'd already accomplished his dream."

All three Hannah boys played for Alabama. Brother Charley is a Raider guard, his third pro position. The brothers grew up in Albertville, Alabama, with a farmer's work ethic. His father built a booming farm supply business from nothing, and John started a 250-acre farm for cattle and chicken in nearby Crossville.

Hannah's teams rarely passed before New England made him the fourth choice in the 1973 draft, so he made himself into a pass blocker. It took some time, but he studied films of successful linemen with similar wide bodies. He practiced their techniques over and over.

With experience, he grew smarter. In his first

few years, if a player beat him a few times early, he said, "I just wasted the whole game being mad." Now, he says, if things aren't going well, "All you can do is take it calmly and think about technique and fundamentals and try to get yourself together."

He learned the best body positions for maximizing his raw strength. He learned how to vary blocking styles to keep opponents guessing. He learned to decide who to block downfield, and who was harmlessly out of the play.

One thing Hannah never had to learn was the value of winning. At Alabama, he said Bear Bryant may not have taught pass blocking, "but he did teach us what it took to win, and what it meant to win." He reinforced the work ethic.

But Hannah's teams never won a national championship in college, or a playoff game in the pros. His Patriots have made the playoffs only three times, and their best chance was in 1978, the year they won the AFC East with an 11-5 record. That team rushed for 3,165 yards, an NFL record, without any one back breaking 800. But after Houston smoked them in the playoffs, Hannah felt betrayed. He said, "Looking back, I don't feel all our players were dedicated enough to go all the way."

His relationship with the Patriots has never been friendly. As Mike Haynes said after leaving New England for the Raiders, "Al Davis spends more on the party after the game than the Patriots spend on winning the game." The Patriots' frugality reached its limit for Hannah before the 1977 season, when he was an all-pro guard scheduled to make a lower salary than his brother, a third-round rookie. His contract, signed when he still couldn't pass block, bound him through 1980 at less than the NFL average. When the Patriots wouldn't improve it, he held out with Leon Gray, a tackle in a similar financial squeeze.

The Patriots traded Gray in 1979. "They might as well forget about the Super Bowl," Hannah said. From there, they struggled through a 2–14 year in 1981 and 2½ strained seasons under Ron

Meyer, the coach Hannah said "hasn't learned that you talk to an older person a little different than a kid." With Raymond Berry coaching his first full season in 1985, Hannah eagerly promised to report in the best shape of his career. "John is unique," Berry said. "He has the rare ability of being extremely intense play after play, game after game. He has a great will to win."

The blocker has to dance with the pass rusher, anticipate his moves, and keep him chest to chest. Hannah follows him all the way, step for step, in a ground-shaking ballet. "Once in awhile he does things that are unbelievable," said former Patriot coach Ron Erhardt.

MIKE HAYNES
MR. PLUCKY

Los Angeles Raiders
Born July 1, 1953, at Denison, Texas
Height, 6.02. Weight, 190.

			INTERCEPTIONS				PUNT RETURNS			
YEAR	CLUB	G	NO	YDS	AVG	TD	NO	YDS	AVG	TD
1976	New England NFL	14	8	90	11.3	0	45	608	13.5	2
1977	New England NFL	14	5	54	10.8	0	24	200	8.3	0
1978	New England NFL	16	6	123	20.5	1	14	183	13.1	0
1979	New England NFL	16	3	66	22.0	0	5	16	3.2	0
1980	New England NFL	13	1	31	31.0	0	17	140	8.2	0
1981	New England NFL	8	1	3	3.0	0	6	12	2.0	0
1982	New England NFL	9	4	26	6.5	0	-	-	-	-
1983	L.A. Raiders NFL	5	1	0	0.0	0	-	-	-	-
1984	L.A. Raiders NFL	16	6	220	28.1	1	-	-	-	-

Mike Haynes likes to get up at the line of scrimmage, nose to nose with wide receivers, where a cornerback has the margin for error of a rock climber. Up there, he says, "I feel in control." Playing on pro football's cutting edge, Haynes grabs the blade from the receiver and whips him with the handle. "It's like you ordered him out of a catalog," says Willie Brown, Haynes's defensive backfield coach with the Los Angeles Raiders and the Hall of Fame cornerback who set the standard for aggressive pass coverage.

"He's big and fast with long arms and legs," Seattle wide receiver Steve Largent says. "He's a smart player. You really can't outwit him. I feel he's the complete cornerback."

Still, man-to-man coverage, especially bumping receivers at the line and running with them, was relatively new to Haynes when he joined the Raiders in 1983. He had made six Pro Bowls in seven seasons at New England, missing only when a collapsed lung forced him out of half the 1981 season. But New England had played mostly zone coverage. Even though Haynes was regarded the NFL's best cornerback, the move to Los Angeles put his reputation on the line. Right where he wanted it. "If I thought I was the world's best, I'd get bored," Haynes says. "Where would the challenge be?"

He fit into the Raiders' defense splendidly. Haynes doesn't have the physical style of their other all-pro cornerback, Lester Hayes, who tries to literally beat receivers into submission. Haynes is more smooth and graceful. He plays the bump-and-run by matching receivers step for step. He has a 37″ inseam, he was a college long jump champ, and Raider safety Vann McElroy says, "He can catch up so fast and jump so high that if he's within four yards of a receiver, the man's basically covered."

Hayes called Haynes's acquisition "a blessing from God." Raider wide receiver Cliff Branch had told owner Al Davis that Haynes was all the team needed to go to the Super Bowl. It already had Hayes, but offenses weren't even bothering to throw in that direction. The Raiders can't get by with mere above-average corners because their attacking style of pass rush and tight coverage makes their corners cover one-on-one. "They want you to disrupt the route the receiver is trying to run," Haynes says.

He didn't play until the last five games. A dispute about whether his trade from New England beat the trading deadline cost him five games. When Haynes finally arrived, he let other people make the point that he was the final piece in the Super Bowl puzzle. Haynes just went to work, happy to do it for a winner. "He's just so nice," linebacker Matt Millen said.

The Raiders made it to the Super Bowl against the Redskins. Washington's first three passes were in Haynes's direction. All were incomplete. With the pass rusher crowding quarterback Joe Theismann and Haynes and Hayes practically smuggling themselves inside the receivers' jerseys, Washington completed only 6 of its first 18 passes. The Raiders pulled ahead early. Theismann went without a touchdown pass for only the second time all season. Haynes made an interception. When the Raiders won 38–9, he said, "It was like no feeling I'd ever had before. It was such a high that if you felt that way all the time, you'd be locked up in an insane asylum and be bouncing off the walls."

After the euphoria wore off, Haynes thought less about how he had proven himself than about how much better he would be after a full year with the Raiders. "I don't go around thinking, I've been playing all these years, I've arrived," he said. "I want to keep learning. I don't try to be better than another guy or as good as another guy. I just try to be as good as I can be. That way, I put no limits on myself."

After the Raiders' 38–9 Super Bowl victory over the Redskins, Haynes said, "It was like no feeling I've ever had before. It was such a high that if you felt that way all the time, you'd be locked up in an insane asylum and be bouncing off the walls."

Haynes knew all about limits. As a youth at Los Angeles's John Marshall High School, he had fenced himself inside a world without aspirations. He could have done well in the state track meet, but first he had to qualify in the city meet, and that was inconveniently the day after prom night. "I didn't have my priorities in line," he says. He also says, "I was a follower." Although the sport he played best was baseball, he stuck to football because that's what his pals played.

"I look back on my life and I realize I didn't have any goals or plans at all when I was a kid," Haynes says. "I wasn't thinking about college at all. All I could see was maybe I'd go to a junior college for two years, play a little more football, and then go to work as a shipping clerk. It's sad, really, looking back."

He had a menial job for a year after high school. The next year, he says, Arizona State coach Frank Kush rescued him from his self-sentence to oblivion. He knows he was lucky. He knows his story has more sad endings than happy ones. "Black kids set such low goals for themselves, like I did," Haynes says. "They have enough sports heroes. They need to believe they can be Lee Iacoccas, too."

What Kush did was stretch Haynes's limits. If he intercepted a pass, Kush said he should have caught the ball at the highest point he could reach it. Next time, the receiver might do that and beat him to it. Haynes started setting goals. As a junior, he wanted to lead the country in interceptions. He did, with 11.

His hands always were good enough to play wide receiver. "I still think he could be an all-pro wide receiver," Raider defensive coach Charlie Sumner says. There has been talk of moving him much of his career, and when he seriously considered the USFL in 1983, he wanted to play both offense and defense. Haynes became a cornerback his freshman year when he filled in for an injured starter and intercepted passes in his first two games. The next year, he would have moved to wide receiver, but Kush recruited a freshman named John Jefferson.

New England drafted Haynes on the fifth pick in 1976. He was Rookie of the Year, he went on to be a perennial all-pro, but something was missing. "I was never convinced winning was a goal there," Haynes says. "Winning costs money, in salaries and such." The Raiders were not only willing to bear the expense of winning, they expected to win. Haynes marveled at his new teammates' casual attitude after they won the game to qualify for the Super Bowl. Clearly, they had put the championship well within their limits.

"I think the only reason I'm able to do what I do is I work so hard to do it," Haynes says. "I try to keep improving. I look for an area to improve." Speed, for one. Most players expect to slow down long before they reach Haynes's age, 32. But Haynes wouldn't accept that. Track coaches told him it wasn't necessary. So he works off-seasons with Arizona State's track team and his 4.4 forty is faster than when he was a rookie.

"You work hard to get people to call you the best, but then when it happens it can be a distraction," he says. "I'd rather people say I'm still improving. I'd like it to be where I'm out of football for 10 years, and then people look back and say, 'Haynes was the best.' "

"He's big and fast with long arms and legs," Seattle wide receiver Steve Largent says. "He's a smart player. You really can't outwit him. I feel he's the complete cornerback."

CHRIS HINTON
LINING UP FOR STARDOM

Indianapolis Colts
Born July 31, 1961, at Chicago, Illinois
Height, 6.04. Weight, 280.

YEAR	CLUB	G
1983	Baltimore NFL	16
1984	Indianapolis NFL	6

It was barely two years after Chris Hinton had been kicked off the worst team in college football history. Now he was starting at left guard in the January 1984 Pro Bowl. He was the first rookie offensive lineman ever to start for the AFC all-stars, the only representative from the soon-to-be-Indianapolis Colts in four years.

The strange thing is, one thing followed the other very logically. At least, it was as logical as possible in a journey that would take Hinton to four cities in three years, four positions in four years.

He called it the turning point of his career when he got kicked off Northwestern's team for 10 days at the beginning of fall practice in 1981. He was a junior then. Two years earlier, he had been one of the country's prize high school recruits, the ballyhooed cornerstone of Northwestern's promised resurgence. Now he was an undistinguished player on a team that would lose 34 straight games, an NCAA record, before going 3–8 in Hinton's junior year. After two winless seasons, Hinton said it was easy to tell himself he was working harder than he had been. He was one of five players to report out of shape. Dennis Green, the new coach, sent them all home.

"I didn't believe he did that," Hinton said, "I felt like calling him every name in the book. I thought maybe he didn't like me. Then I realized if he didn't like me, he would have just kept me around and not played me.

"Even when I came back, I didn't start until the third game. That really blew my mind. I said, 'Hey, things aren't as easy as I thought.' "

When it came time to draft Hinton's class a year and a half later, scouts were impressed by his work habits, his hustle. They saw how he chased down punts, beating all his teammates but the fastest wide receiver. They saw how he put out for a 1–10 team as a senior. "It didn't matter what the score was," Green said. "We could be leading 17–10 or trailing 30–0. He gave everything on every play."

Hinton was impressive to meet, too. "He's the kind of kid who walks into a room and everything lights up," says Doc Glass, a longtime adviser to Northwestern athletes. He has a big smile that seems to sneak up and take over his face, as though he can't help it.

But Hinton impressed scouts most as an athlete. "For a big man, he was able to make a fundamental mistake and recover to save the play," said Hal Hunter, then the Colts' offensive line coach. Even off-balance, Hinton was athletic enough to make most blocks.

"He's one of those rare people that possess exceptional athletic skills and play offensive line," said Jim Finks, then Chicago's general manager. Even the best offensive linemen are rarely good all-around athletes. They don't run the hurdles or pitch shutouts or clear the offensive boards. They're big, strong, usually smart, and very good at one thing. They keep better athletes, defensive linemen, from going where they want to go.

But Hinton had lettered in wrestling, track, and basketball at Phillips High School in Chicago. In football, he was too good an athlete to waste on

the offensive line until it became clear he could become one of the greatest linemen ever. Northwestern used him at linebacker and tight end until his senior year. Then he bulked up from 235 pounds to 275 without losing a tick off his 4.8-second time for 40 yards. Hinton would miss catching passes, but Green said, "He made up his mind to be the best tackle in the country."

Before that season, Green said, "If he has the type of year he can have, I think he's going to be drafted in the first few rounds." He still wasn't regarded a first-rounder at the end of the season, although he was Northwestern's MVP, an all-America, and on the all-America strength team. Green had to beg people to put him in the college all-star games for seniors. He was a late addition to the most important one, the Senior Bowl.

That was where Hinton bowled over the scouts, to say nothing of would-be tacklers. "He can run. He can change directions. He's got balance," Finks said. "He's head and shoulders above most college linemen." He had the strength to open near canyons of running room. And as a pass blocker, he had protected the prime pass-rush corridor as left tackle in the Michigan game, when Northwestern passed 71 times without a sack.

On draft day, Hinton was the fourth player chosen, by Denver. The Broncos toasted him as the NFL's best lineman of the next decade. Then they traded him to the Colts for John Elway.

"He has quick feet and the size to hold off the inside rush," Green said. "Those are the two main things in pass blocking."

"All this after just one year as a lineman. Hinton would only get better," scouts said. Suddenly, he was a high first-round prospect. Too high, in one sense. Hinton was a homebody from a close, religious family. He wanted to play for the Bears, who had the sixth pick. They wanted him. But it was looking like he would go in the top five. He was too good, an irony of exhilaration and frustration for someone whose college teams had gone 4–40.

Hinton lived in the suburbs until, for his freshman year in high school, the family moved to a house it owned on the South Side. There, he went to an inner city school without a locker room. Football players dressed at home, walked to a public park four blocks from school, and hoped nobody would hurt himself on the rocks, bricks, and broken glass. To Hinton's relief, the street gangs respected athletes. "They let me go my own way," he said.

On draft day, Hinton was the fourth player chosen, by Denver. The Broncos toasted him as the NFL's best lineman of the next decade. But looking back, Hinton suspects they never intended to keep him. They might even already have made the trade that would send quarterback John Elway to Denver and Hinton to the Colts, then still in Baltimore.

The trade itself didn't bother him. Offensive linemen are used to going where they're told. "What bothered me was the way it was done. I wasn't notified until after I'd heard about it through the media, and it was conditional on whether Elway signed with Denver. It had nothing to do with me."

As a rookie, Hinton started every game but the opener. He was the best blocker on the NFL's second best rushing team. The Colts, 0–8–1 in 1982, improved to 6–4 before finishing 7–9. "Whenever we needed a yard or two, we went to Chris's side," Colt quarterback Mike Pagel said. "From day one, he controlled the line of scrimmage. During the season, we'd throw in some new things and he'd pick them up right away."

The Colts were desperate for help at left tackle last season, so Hinton moved back to his college position until he broke his leg in the sixth game. Without their blocking anchor, the Colts went 4–12 in Hinton's tumultuous second season. Coach Frank Kush resigned before the last game. But things were settling down when he went to the team's minicamp in May, able to run again. Hinton was glad to hear new coach Rod Dowhower was penciling him in at guard again for 1985. "I prefer to play guard," he said. "But the challenge of making the Pro Bowl at a different position is sort of intriguing."

RICKEY JACKSON
GOBBLING UP BIG PLAYS

New Orleans Saints
Born March 20, 1958, at Pahokee, Florida
Height, 6.02. Weight, 236.

YEAR	CLUB	G	SACKS
1981	New Orleans NFL	16	8
1982	New Orleans NFL	9	4½
1983	New Orleans NFL	16	11
1984	New Orleans NFL	16	12

Twice as a senior in college, Rickey Jackson sacked a punter. He didn't even give the guy enough time to *try* a kick. Jackson has that kind of speed, that kind of instinct. More than anything, though, Jackson has that kind of desperation to be the player fans talk about while they walk through the parking lot.

Jackson's hunger for recognition has served him well. He has fed it by chewing up ball carriers and spitting out the laces. He has enjoyed the national spotlight of the last two Pro Bowls. But before that could happen, he had to learn to keep his eyes on the plate in front of him.

There were times, in his first two NFL seasons, when Jackson would go for the big play and give up an even bigger one. He was playing for the New Orleans Saints, the first losing team in his career. His teammates weren't making many big plays, so Jackson would just have to make them all himself. He played out of control, as coaches put it. At the slightest opportunity for a sack or an interception, he ignored his assignment. He was feeding himself to the lions. Experienced quarterbacks and running backs take advantage of reckless abandon.

"He's learned from his experiences," Saints linebacker Jim Kovach says. "The plays he makes now are great plays. He still free-lances, but he's a lot smarter about it. He's learned to pick his spots."

Jackson's 11 sacks in 1983 and 12 in 1984 led not only the Saints, but all NFL linebackers. He no longer had to choke back his pride. "I know I'm one of the best players in the league," he said. The Saints' defense ranked second and then fourth in yards allowed, and first both years in passing yards, but it still gave up too many points. The team still had gone 18 years without a winning season. "I think we can be the No. 1 defense," Jackson said, "and not just on stats. I think we can be No. 1 when it counts, when it's time to rise to the occasion. That's what the winners do."

For the first time in his life, Jackson was the star of his team.

He hadn't been in college. Pitt had the No. 1 defense in the country, but Hugh Green played for that defense, too. Green was a serious candidate for the Heisman Trophy in 1980, when he and Jackson were seniors. The forest of publicity cranked out on Green's behalf only obscured Jackson more. "Nobody appreciates me in Pittsburgh," he said as Green got more and more glory while Jackson made more and more plays. Teams were afraid to run to Green's side, and Jackson was the other defensive end. In the Gator Bowl, against South Carolina and Heisman winner George Rogers, Jackson made 19 tackles.

Even in high school, Jackson was the other guy on the defensive line. His Pahokee High teams played in three Florida state championship games, and the school won a state championship in basketball, but the player they talked about in parking lots, barbershops and taverns was Remuise Johnson, a local legend.

Johnson was Jackson's friend, as Green would be later. When Johnson turned to preaching instead of college ball, Jackson wore his high school number under his own Pitt jersey. But it galled him to be an afterthought. Pahokee, 45 miles inland from Palm Beach, had 6,000 people, and Jackson said, "Not one ever said I'd make it."

That helps explain the ruckus Jackson has raised over his contract with the Saints. Before the 1984 season, the Saints renegotiated the unfair deal he had signed as a rookie in 1981. But one year later, Jackson was stomping his foot again, threatening to sit out the season, saying "This year I want financial security for life or else," and generally prompting fans to talk about him in heated voices. Most of them didn't understand that money was not the issue—at least not in the sense that fans think of money, as something useful for buying groceries and gasoline. Pro athletes' salaries have gone way beyond that.

They have become status symbols. Where high school and college players count each others' stars on a locker room chart or merit decals on their helmets, NFL players compare salaries. When Jackson compared his $300,000 for 1985 with Green's $500,000 and Lawrence Taylor's $650,000, he felt unappreciated again, although a

Jackson developed his speed by chasing rabbits through the fields of Pahokee, Florida, where he was raised, a place so small "you could put the whole town in one of those U.S. Steel buildings."

look at his roots suggests he doesn't consider money's purchasing power merely incidental.

Pahokee is a rural town where whites live in homes from *Gone with the Wind* and blacks live in wood shacks without doors. Jackson has told of corners in his neighborhood that look like dope-sellers' conventions. At Pittsburgh, he said Pahokee was "so small, you could put the whole town in one of those U.S. Steel buildings downtown. But I think we've got more whorehouses in Pahokee than in all Pittsburgh."

His parents divorced before Rickey started school, and his mother supported eight children driving a school bus. One way Jackson developed his speed was chasing rabbits through the fields.

Rabbit was one of his basic dinners. The blacks worked in either the fields or the sugar mills. Strong young men could make money at the corn packing plant, lifting boxes that weighed at least 40 pounds more than 2,000 times a day. Pahokee High's football coach never had to bother with a weightlifting program.

Jackson developed an awesome match of strength and quickness. "He's got such quick hands and quick feet," Saints tight end Hoby Brenner says, "it's hard to engage him with your block."

When he was in fourth grade, Jackson was the starting nose tackle on Pahokee's junior high team until school officials decided that sort of child labor was intolerable. But they couldn't take the football out of the kid. That was when Jackson started dreaming of making it in the NFL. He was going to break free from the poverty he had seen squeeze the hearts out of so many neighbors. He called Pahokee "a town of losers."

"To get out," Jackson said, "you've got to tell yourself over and over that you're a winner. I didn't want to wind up like those wineheads in the streets. I didn't want to get stuck in the fields. You work in the fields for 10 years—if you're 30, you look 60. I convinced myself that I was going to be the best around and that nothing could stop me. Everything I did was a surprise to the people down there."

It hasn't been enough yet. To Jackson, reaching the top was just a necessary step in his long-range plan. The great ones stay there. "Used to be is like death to me," Jackson says.

"He might not have a lot of book knowledge, " said Rogers, who became his best friend on the Saints, "but common sense is his greatest asset."

Rogers was the first pick in the 1981 draft. Green was the seventh. Jackson figured he would be claimed soon after them. But he had to wait. And wait. The second round was almost over when the Saints made him the draft's 51st pick. He had been overlooked again.

"I just need a chance to play," Jackson said. "That's all I ask. I'll try to bring New Orleans from the bottom to the top. Just like I've done the rest of my life. From the bottom to the top. I'm used to that."

DAVE KRIEG
MILTON'S PARADISE FOUND

Seattle Seahawks
Born October 20, 1958, at Iola, Wisconsin
Height, 6.01. Weight, 185.

YEAR	CLUB	G	ATT	CMP	PASSING PCT	GAIN	TO	INT	AVG	RUSHING ATT	YDS	AVG	TD
1980	Seattle NFL	1	2	0	00.0	0	0	0	0.00	-	-	-	-
1981	Seattle NFL	7	112	64	57.1	843	7	5	7.53	11	56	5.1	1
1982	Seattle NFL	3	78	49	62.8	501	2	2	6.42	6	-3	-0.5	0
1983	Seattle NFL	9	243	147	60.5	2139	18	11	8.80	16	55	3.4	2
1984	Seattle NFL	16	480	276	57.5	3671	32	24	7.65	46	186	4.0	3

The name was pronounced Craig. That was something the Seattle Seahawks had to keep pointing out. Even after Dave Krieg was the NFL's fourth-rated passer in 1983, a starting quarterback in the AFC championship game, he was no better known than a lacrosse star. Usually, quarterbacks follow their reputations into the NFL. Krieg followed only his dream.

Even now, Krieg is known more for where he has played than how well he has played. He's that guy from the little school that folded. His alma mater, Milton College, went out of business in 1981, the year after Krieg graduated. "I won't get a football field named after me," he says. "Then again, I won't have to pay alumni dues, either."

The NFL is only beginning to take Krieg more seriously than he does. It's hard to ignore his results, even if it's obvious he doesn't have the nightly news-clip passing style of Dan Fouts, Joe Montana, or Dan Marino. All Krieg does is throw touchdown passes and win games.

Since he became the starting quarterback in mid-1983, the Seahawks have gone 17–7, plus 3–2 in playoff games. He has thrown touchdown passes in 24 of 25 games, including the last 18. He had the NFL's highest touchdown percentage in 1983 and trailed only Marino in 1984, when his total of 32 was the fifth highest ever against NFL defensive backs. And he doesn't just heave the ball downfield, come what may. His completion percentage for the last two years is .585, and he has blemished his 50 touchdowns with only 35 interceptions.

"He's a big-play quarterback," Seahawk wide

receiver Steve Largent says. "He's not real flashy or a pinpoint passer like Fouts, but he'll make the plays for you."

In Seattle's first playoff ever, the wild card game in 1983, Krieg helped beat Denver 31–7 with 12-for-13 passing for 200 yards and three touchdowns. The next week, after his interception allowed Miami to go ahead, Krieg bounced back with passes for 16 and 40 yards on the 66-yard drive to the winning touchdown with 1:52 to play. In the Seahawks' biggest 1984 game, the one that tied them for first place, he completed 30 of 44 for 406 yards and three touchdowns against a Denver defense that had given up nine touchdown passes in 12 games.

But even his coach didn't seem to believe it. After the 1983 season, Chuck Knox tried hard to sign Canadian all-star Warren Moon. Last off-season, he went after Dieter Brock and Bobby Hebert.

To hear Krieg talk, the Seahawks better find someone in a hurry. "I don't think I have any one quality that is outstanding," he says. "I just go out and try to do whatever it takes. If that means I complete passes, OK. If it means I have to scramble, I try and scramble. I don't want to make the job too complicated. I hand off, and sometimes I throw. People give me a lot more credit than I deserve."

Krieg always wants to be able to fit his head in his small Wisconsin hometown. Football is big there. The glory-day Packers have practically been made into dashboard statuettes. "But when you're there awhile, you blend in again," Krieg says. "That's what I like about small towns. If I had to do it all over again, I'd still go to Milton College."

At the time, he didn't have a lot of alternatives. Krieg played for a power-I team at Everest High School in Schofield, near his Rothschild home in north central Wisconsin. His team didn't pass much more often than it dropkicked. But his high school coach had played for Rudy Gaddini, who had moved on to Milton, in southern Wisconsin. At least Gaddini used a pro-style offense. Krieg went there with a $500 scholarship.

Milton had 237 students, 175 of them males. Seven of them were trying out for quarterback. Krieg won the job in his fifth game. As a senior, he was the seventh-ranked passer in the NAIA. Gaddini had another good friend, Seattle personnel director Dick Mansperger, so he wrote a letter that fall. "If it wasn't for that, Krieg says, "I'd probably be working at the Weyerhauser paper mill back home. Or Roto-Rooter maybe."

Unlike most pro quarterbacks, Krieg didn't come out of a big university. His alma mater was Milton College, in Wisconsin, a little-known, now-defunct school with 237 students, 175 of them male. And eight of them trying out for the quarterback's job.

Krieg was one of 55 undrafted rookies in Seattle's 1980 training camp. "It was neat to see a professional locker room," he says. "I wasn't worried. I was just looking for a chance to stay around." It came after the other three rookie quarterbacks had been cut. Krieg had to beat out only one veteran. When Steve Meyer was injured, he says, "There I was, an NFL quarterback. It was hard to believe."

It was time to go to work, to decipher the hieroglyphics of NFL defenses. "I didn't have time to say, 'Gee whiz, I'm a quarterback in the NFL,' " he says. "I was never in awe of this, really. Everything was magnified, playing in this league, but it's still a 100-yard field. It's still just a football game."

Krieg's first extended playing time came November 1, 1981, at Green Bay, of all places. His fairy godmother took the day off. It would be nice to say he set the hometown team on its ear, but in Krieg's nine minutes, he threw an interception and the Packers' lead grew from 28–24 to 34–24. "Maybe there will be another time," he said.

It came soon. Quarterback Jim Zorn broke his ankle with three games left. Seattle was a prohibitive underdog in Krieg's first start, against the playoff-bound Jets and their league-leading pass rush. But he completed 20 of 26 passes with two touchdowns. "There are more guys in front of my locker here than in the stands at Milton," he told reporters. The 6–10 Seahawks went 2–1 in Krieg's starts. He was ready to challenge Zorn, the local hero who had started six seasons for Seattle. As far as Krieg was concerned, Milton was no longer an issue.

"A lot of fellas go to training camps with no notoriety and make clubs as free agents," he said. "So much of it is timing. I just happened to be in the right place when the opportunity arose. But when you get it, you better use it."

Krieg won the starting job in 1982, but it lasted two games. Coach Jack Patera was fired during the strike, and Krieg's job went with him. He didn't get it back until the eighth 1983 game, when Seattle was 4–3 and trailing Pittsburgh 24–0 at halftime. Krieg threw two second-half touchdown passes and the Steelers had to sweat out a 27–21 victory. Starting the next week, he beat the Raiders with touchdowns on two passes and one run.

"He doesn't get ruffled," quarterback coach Ken Meyer said. "He's a leader. There's a certain way you're going to wiggle your butt when you get up to the line of scrimmage. Everybody sees it and says, 'This guy is going to take charge.' "

After the 1983 season, Krieg was able to trade in his old Pinto for a BMW. His salary rose from $85,000 to more than $250,000, still a bargain. But his feet stayed on the ground. It was no time to stop making himself better. For example, he said, "I'd like to throw the ball where I'm aiming it. You have to be consistent and play a few years. You've got to do it year after year, three or four years in a row." That's what he plans. But he also knows this: "Whatever I do will be more than anyone expected."

"He's a big-play quarterback," says Krieg's receiver, Steve Largent. "He's not real flashy or a pinpoint passer like Fouts, but he'll make the plays for you." Says Krieg, "Whatever I do will be more than anyone expected."

STEVE LARGENT
MOVIN' ON UP

Seattle Seahawks
Born September 28, 1954, at Tulsa, Oklahoma
Height, 5.11. Weight, 184.

| | | | PASS RECEIVING | | | |
YEAR	CLUB	G	NO	YDS	AVG	TD
1976	Seattle NFL	14	54	705	13.0	4
1977	Seattle NFL	14	33	643	19.5	10
1978	Seattle NFL	16	71	1168	16.5	8
1979	Seattle NFL	15	66	1237	18.7	9
1980	Seattle NFL	16	66	1064	16.1	6
1981	Seattle NFL	16	75	1224	16.3	9
1982	Seattle NFL	8	34	493	14.5	3
1983	Seattle NFL	15	72	1074	14.9	11
1984	Seattle NFL	16	74	1164	15.7	12

After he became Seattle's coach, one of Chuck Knox's pleasant surprises was finding out just what a gold mine he had in wide receiver Steve Largent. He hadn't realized it. Largent's greatness doesn't leap off the field at you. He doesn't outrace long passes, shifting into hyperthrust like some receivers. He's more subtle, not to mention more slow.

But somehow, Largent has been able to gather up enough speed for six 1,000-yard seasons in the nine he has played. The NFL record is seven. He ranks third all-time in 100-yard games, with 32. The only other player with more than 10 touchdown catches the last two seasons was Roy Green, who wouldn't lose a race to Largent unless he stopped for lunch.

"He's one of the best," says Denver cornerback Louis Wright, who has tried to cover Largent twice a year since 1976. But why? Even Largent's own receivers coach, Steve Moore, says "It's hard to analyze why." He tries, though, and comes up with a sensible explanation. Largent plays within his limits, but not very far within them. "Steve has developed his skills. His shortcomings, he doesn't worry about," Moore says.

Largent knows he'll never run a 4.3 forty, so he

has worked on becoming the best move maker in football. He has honed his concentration so it will cut through rain, sleet, and helmets to the ribs. He has studied defenses to the point where, quarterback Dave Krieg says, "He brings a lot of good information back to the huddle. He doesn't just think of himself. He's seeing how other receivers can get open."

He is a poet among panzers. If his greatness goes largely unnoticed, it's for the same reason people don't seek out marching bands to hear flutes play.

"I think I've always been an overachiever," Largent says. "The thing that motivates me more than anything else is people telling me I can't do something, that I'm too slow or too small to play wide receiver. That just makes me work harder."

He does his work one step at a time. Largent didn't think about playing college ball when he was in high school, and he says the NFL was never an ambition. "I sort of take life as a day-to-day proposition," he says. "I never set long-range goals. That's the way I look at the records and all the rest. I just worry about getting through practice. After that, I start thinking about how to get home."

He beats cornerbacks with the same single-minded concentration. Literally, one step at a time. He can cut without slowing down, Seahawk quarterback coach Ken Meyer says. "He's never out of control or off-balance. That allows him to make his breaks and moves quickly."

Largent's teammates call him Yoda because he is a master at making cornerbacks commit themselves, at baiting their traps. "He's a master of forcing you to turn on him," Seahawk cornerback Dave Brown says. "His moves are so solid that you can't ignore them. You have to turn and go, and he beats you when you turn."

It's the quickness of his second move that sets him free. Or the third, if he needs it. What distinguishes Largent is the body control to make that second move while the cornerback is still reacting to his first move. "It happens all the time to everybody," Brown says.

He can make his legs go one way and his upper body go another way," says Jim Zorn, Seattle's back-up quarterback.

"He's the best athlete I ever played with," Krieg says.

Jerry Rhome, a longtime Seattle offensive coach now with the Redskins, says Largent's body control is even more impressive when the ball is in the air. That's when he bends and twists to catch it. He doesn't wait for the ball to come to

Largent's teammates call him "Yoda" because he is a master at making cornerbacks commit themselves, at baiting their traps. "He's a master of forcing you to turn on him," Seahawk cornerback Dave Brown says. "You have to turn and go, and he beats you when you turn."

him. "Let's say the ball's just a little short," Rhome says. "Largent can stop, come back, and make the play. I'd rather have a guy like Largent, who can change directions, than the fastest guy in the world."

The best example of doing one thing at a time is concentration. Largent works on that, too. He has learned that concentration increases as the focal area decreases. So he doesn't try to concentrate on the whole ball. He concentrates on just the tip. It's his most important asset, Largent says, because "Whether you catch the ball or not is the bottom line of everything a receiver does."

Largent has caught enough balls for six 50-catch seasons, one short of the NFL record. No other active player has five. Largent was the first NFL wide receiver in the 1970s to catch 70 passes and to gain 1,200 yards. He has caught passes in

107 straight games, the third-best streak ever and 20 short of Harold Carmichael's record. His 458 catches in the last seven years are the most in the NFL, an average of 69 catches per 16-game season. That puts him within two seasons of Charlie Joiner's career record 657 catches, although Joiner is still playing. Largent is the only receiver among the all-time top 20 with fewer than 10 seasons.

Largent conceivably could play 16 years, as Joiner has. The strengths of his game tend to improve with experience. But he won't hang on to pad statistics. He says, "If I'm not good enough to be throwing to me all the time, to attract double coverages, then that's when I'll know my usefulness is gone."

Two years ago, Largent was planning to retire after 1984. He was tired of losing. The Seahawks had surprising 9–7 seasons in 1978 and 1979, but they won just 14 games in the next three years, and never more than 10 in a season. "It was very unfulfilling," he says.

That began changing in 1983, when Largent's two straight catches set up the two-yard touchdown run that upset Miami in the playoffs. But that was a wild-card team that got hot late. Last year was a whole season at 12–4. In the 13th game, Seattle played Denver for first place. Largent had the best game of his career in Seattle's 27–24 victory: 12 catches, 191 yards, and a touchdown.

"Just to play in a game like this does something to you," he said. "In the old days I'd sit at home, watching everyone else in the playoffs, and I'd think, 'Hey, I'm as good as that guy.' It was very discouraging.

He made all-pro for the third time in 1983 and his fourth Pro Bowl last year. Winning brought some national attention. "People assume you must be playing a lot better than you used to," he said. "I think I'm pretty much like I've always been, but everything around me has changed."

Largent has been a rare constant since Seattle's first season, 1976. The Oilers drafted him in the fourth round that year, but they were happy to unload him for an eighth-round pick. Seattle was happy to get him. Rhome had just moved to Seattle's new staff from Tulsa, where Largent had led the country with 14 touchdown catches the last two years. Even so, he wasn't in much more demand than he had been at Putnam City High School in Oklahoma City. Too slow, the scouts said.

Rhome knew better. Rhome knew the wisdom of Tulsa coach F. A. Dry, whose words are still appropriate. "If you're looking for a sprinter, he's not that," Dry said. "If you're looking for a wide receiver, he is that."

Although Largent isn't known for his speed, he ranks third all-time in 100-yard games, with 32. The only other player with more than ten touchdown catches the last two seasons was Roy Green, who wouldn't lose a race to Largent unless he stopped for lunch.

LOUIS LIPPS
MANY HAPPY RETURNS

Pittsburgh Steelers
Born August 9, 1962, at New Orleans, Louisiana
Height, 5.10. Weight, 190.

YEAR	CLUB	G	PASS RECEIVING				PUNT RETURNS				RUSHING			
			NO	YDS	AVG	TD	NO	YDS	AVG	TD	ATT	YDS	AVG	TD
1984	Pittsburgh NFL	14	45	860	19.1	9	53	656	12.4	1	3	71	23.7	1

Sending Louis Lipps back to return punts last season was like picking up Three Rivers Stadium and shaking it. The Pittsburgh Steeler fans stretched their lungs. They chanted, "Lou! Lou! Lou! Lou!" They braced for excitement.

"It's really something when everyone in the stadium calls your name," Lipps said. "It's like a cold breeze going through you. It's unreal."

As usual, Lipps was speaking softly. Unless he's trying to penetrate the roar of a crowd, Lipps is as reserved off the field as he is electrifying on it. In a day when first-round draft choices have higher profiles than Times Square, Lipps is a walking curfew.

He spent his bonus money on a conservative home in a middle-class neighborhood, not a swinging uptown condo. The fancy new car he bought was a Jeep with four-wheel drive. His agent in contract talks was the family minister.

When the rest of Pittsburgh was comparing him with Lynn Swann, Lipps was saying, "As far as I know, I have a long way to go. I just try to make progress every day."

"Louis is very mature for his age," said 32-year-old John Stallworth, Lipps's running mate at wide receiver. "He's going to be one of the great ones ever to play the game. He already does a lot well and he's only going to get better with the talent he has."

In 1984, Lipps led all rookie receivers with 860 yards. His 19.1-yard average gain led all AFC receivers with more than 35 catches. He finished within 11 yards and an official's gaffe of breaking the NFL record for punt return yardage. His presence helped Stallworth have his best season and the Steelers climb from 27th to 15th on the NFL passing chart. They finished 9–7 and went to their first AFC championship game in five years.

Lipps was the consensus AFC Rookie of the Year, the Pro Bowl punt returner, and Mississippi's Professional Athlete of the Year for a year another native, Walter Payton, became the NFL's all-time rushing champ. He was the only NFL player to score touchdowns rushing, receiving, and returning a kick. His 85-yard punt return was the longest of the season and the Steelers' first for a touchdown in 10 years. His 1,587 all-purpose yards led all rookies. Four of his nine touchdown catches went at least 61 yards.

"He's so dangerous after he catches the ball," Steeler quarterback Mark Malone said. "You can get him the ball seven, eight, ten yards downfield, and it can turn into an 80-yard play."

Growing up in Reserve, Louisiana, where he played split end and defensive back at East St. John's High, Lipps didn't think a college coach would find him, let alone the NFL. Reserve is a Mississippi River Delta town, southeast of New Orleans, that would fit in the Superdome. Lipps calls it Blink City, as in, "Blink your eyes on the way through it and you miss it." But Southern Mississippi found him. He caught 91 passes there, 40 for 800 yards as a senior, and ranked in the country's top 13 punt returners his last two seasons. The fans called him "Hot Lipps."

The Steelers rated him the fifth best player in the 1984 draft. They were stunned to see him available on their turn, 23rd in the first round. Lipps proved them right by making 45 catches as a rookie. The three wideouts who were drafted ahead of him caught 37 among them.

Lipps made a splash in his first game, when he replaced injured starter Calvin Sweeney. He caught six passes for 183 yards and two touchdowns. On his 80-yard score, he leaped over a defender and then shrugged off a safety trying to tackle him.

That flair for the spectacular invited comparisons with Swann, another high leaper and punt returner. Lipps had a 4.48-second 40 time and a 38-inch vertical jump. He used them both well, as on a 62-yard touchdown play against Indianapolis, Lipps soared between two defenders, tipped the ball with one hand, caught with the other, and took off before anyone could catch him.

"It was like the old days with Swann and Stallworth," veteran Steeler linebacker Jack Lambert said. "[Terry] Bradshaw could throw the ball with confidence. He could wing it up there and those guys would come down with it. You can do that with Louis because he has the same kind of ability."

That was nice for people to say, Lipps said. He accepted the comparisons as compliments, but he figured they contained less fact than flattery.

"Louis is very mature for his age," said John Stallworth, Lipps's running mate at wide receiver. "He's going to be one of the great ones."

"There is probably not going to be another Lynn Swann to come through the NFL," he said, "I put that kind of talk in the back of my mind. I play my type of game and don't try to follow in anyone's footsteps."

In some ways, Lipps's game is better. "Lynn didn't have the strength of a Louis Lipps," Steeler coach Chuck Noll said. "He didn't have that durability." Swann didn't have Lipps' instant success, either. He caught 11 passes as a rookie reserve.

"Louis has the speed to go deep," Noll says. "He is able to catch the ball and run. He can come in on a hook and make people miss him. He has quickness and great acceleration."

His season wasn't all downhill, though. He fumbled six times in his first two games. After five games, he missed two with a sprained ankle and didn't start the next five, although he played on passing downs. He returned to the lineup against San Diego with seven catches for 118 yards and a touchdown. He had four touchdown catches in his last five games and, now concentrating better, fumbled only twice after the first two.

"You don't see him make too many errors anymore," Malone said late in the season. "He's running the right routes, making the right adjustments, and making big plays."

Some of Lipps's biggest plays were on punts. His 12.4-yard average was the league's third best. Late in the Steelers' last game, his 656 return yards were 10 short of the NFL record by Greg Pruitt, who was on the opposing Raiders' bench. He had taken one fair catch in 52 attempts. This last punt came in low. Lipps had a chance for the record. But as he ran, the field judge blew his whistle, saying Lipps had signaled for a fair catch when he raised his left hand, as film later showed, about to waist level. The league changed the fair catch rule in the off-season, requiring the returner's hand to be not only over his head, but also waving.

Lipps didn't blame the official. He recalled recent returns of 73 and 61 yards that had been called back for penalties. His rookie total was just a stepping stone anyway.

The Steelers want Lipps to keep returning punts, even though it is football's most dangerous job and he is integral to their offense. Lipps is all for it. He likes the job. "Punt returns put you into the spotlight," he says. "Everybody watches you. It fires up the crowd. Stadiums go crazy. It picks up the momentum." Especially when the returns go 20 yards or more, as Lipps did 20 times.

"Lipps is dangerous," Noll says. "He's a threat to score from anywhere. Often, he gets one block and that's all he needs."

At Southern Mississippi, Lipps caught 91 passes, 40 for 800 yards as a senior, and ranked in the country's top 13 punt returners his last two seasons. The fans called him "Hot Lipps."

JAMES LOFTON
HANDS ON THE RUN

Green Bay Packers
Born July 5, 1956, at Fort Ord, California
Height, 6.03. Weight, 197.

| | | | PASS RECEIVING | | | |
YEAR	CLUB	G	NO	YDS	AVG	TD
1978	Green Bay NFL	16	46	818	17.8	6
1979	Green Bay NFL	15	54	968	17.9	4
1980	Green Bay NFL	16	71	1226	17.3	4
1981	Green Bay NFL	16	71	1294	18.2	8
1982	Green Bay NFL	9	35	696	19.9	4
1983	Green Bay NFL	16	58	1300	22.4	8
1984	Green Bay NFL	16	62	1361	22.0	7

What makes James Lofton almost unfair is that he doesn't play like a fast receiver. He *runs* like one. His 4.3 time for 40 yards is still one of the top half dozen in the NFL. But fast receivers are supposed to be just that. They're fast. They fly through college without needing any other skills, so they don't develop them.

It isn't enough that Lofton looks like he was built from a kit for wide receivers. Tall. Strong enough to bench press close to twice his weight. Not only fast, but agile and quick. Better hands than a Swiss watch. He's a two-legged jungle cat, with a jaguar's grace and a lion's regal bearing. But he's more. He's also a technician.

He doesn't just race under a long pass and let the ball hit him in the hands. He takes his hands where the ball is going. At full stride, Lofton can adjust his body to the ball's flight. It's beautiful from a distance, but from the opponent's sideline, Lofton is frightening.

"Just watching him line up makes you worry," Viking coach Bud Grant says. "I've seen a few guys with great hands. I don't know if I've ever seen anybody else with his hands, his size, his speed, and his athletic ability."

He is one of the best athletes in the league. His scholarship at Stanford was for track. He was the NCAA long jump champion, and he also qualified for the NCAA meet in 100, 200, and 400 meters. His 27'0" jump was the world's longest in 1977. He has played free safety for the Packers and he has been their emergency quarterback. That was his position at Washington High in Los Angeles, where he grew up with his father after his parents divorced when he was seven. On his only college play at safety, he intercepted a pass.

The last three years, Lofton has ranked third, first, and first in NFL yardage per catch. He's dangerous on the ground, too. His 23 runs in those three years, mostly end arounds, have averaged 9.5 yards. The memory that prodded many NFL fans through the 1982 strike was Lofton's picturesque 83-yard touchdown romp in the last game before the lights went out.

"Any time you get him the ball, you've got a potential touchdown," says his Green Bay Packer offensive coordinator, Bob Schnelker. "He runs under control, and he runs intelligently. But if it's going to be a footrace, there aren't many people who have a chance to catch him."

So defenses try to take away Lofton's long catches. They're the ones that hurt the most. Sometimes they succeed. That's why Lofton works at painting the short strokes as well as the broad strokes. He can catch the curls and quick sideline passes, too. He has caught a pass in all but one of his 89 NFL games. He has been to all but one of seven possible Pro Bowls. After the Packers traded him in 1981 for John Jefferson, then regarded the game's consummate receiver, Lofton received the most all-pro votes of any offensive player.

"The best thing about this guy is that he plays the way he practices," Schnelker says. "Every

"Just watching him line up makes you worry," Viking coach Bud Grant says. "I've seen a few guys with great hands. I don't konw if I've ever seen anybody else with his hands, his size, his speed, and his athletic ability."

Lofton has said he would have liked to be Bill Cosby if he couldn't have been James Lofton: he lists his hobbies as earthquake study, whale watching, and baby bouncing.

play in practice is a precision thing for him. Which is why he does it that way so often in the game."

He's very particular about the way he catches a ball. Just catching it isn't enough. Lofton has to catch it away from his body. There are receivers who prefer to use their bodies, to help them secure the ball when a tackler tries to pop it loose, but Lofton would rather be sure he catches it first. "Usually you have to get to the ball before a defensive back does," he says. "You have to reach out for it. And that means you have to catch the ball in your hands."

That is easier for Lofton because his hands are so big. One time he caught the ball in his right hand and raised it over his head in the same motion, still one-handed.

He doesn't touch a football in the off-season. Many receivers carry one around. They don't like to lose the feel of it. But Lofton has thought this notion through, too. Before a receiver catches the ball, he has to get to it. For that, he needs to go to training camp with his legs in shape. "When those two-a-day practices hit, you see a lot of guys get tired," Lofton says. "They start dragging through practice, sloughing around, getting sloppy with their receiving techniques. My goal is to be in top shape so that all through camp I can work on the small things."

Lofton's intelligence impressed Packer quarterback Lynn Dickey even before his speed. He had been on the team two days when he was answering all the coaches' questions in meetings. "I've never seen a rookie pick up things as fast as he did," Dickey said. His wife, Beverly, didn't know

he also played pro football until she had known him six weeks. She happened to notice the trophies at his father's house.

Among football players, many of whose attention spans are strained by a fortune cookie, Lofton first came across as an aloof egghead. Stereotypes don't account for a smart, businesslike man with the heart of a little boy, who goes to work with a briefcase in one hand and a lunch pail with monster pictures in the other. Lofton has said he would have liked to be Bill Cosby if he couldn't have been James Lofton. His wry sense of humor shows up even in Packer media guides, where his listed hobbies have included earthquake study, whale watching, and baby bouncing.

When Lofton signed a new contract in 1983, the Packers asked him how he would like to announce it. He looked out a window and said, "I guess it's too cold to have a parade." After his first practice under Forrest Gregg, the new coach who brought back grass drills last summer, Lofton said, "Which one was he?" When reporters asked him for a one-word appraisal, he said, "Is cream puff one word or two?"

The image of Lofton's aloofness hasn't held water since 1979, a decidedly unfunny season. The Packers went 5-11, Lofton's temper flared, he lashed out at the fans and coach Bart Starr, and he missed out on the Pro Bowl. His peaceful life suddenly had ripples. Lofton had gone from a winning college team, as the sixth pick in the 1978 draft, to an 8-7 Packer team that was in the playoff race all season. He was the NFC's offensive Rookie of the Year with 46 catches for 818 yards, and six touchdowns, compared to 53, 834, and 4 yards for the rest of Packers' receivers. In 1979, he said, "All I was doing was rebelling against losing."

Then came Beverly, an aspiring actress and model from Arkansas who has sung several pregame national anthems. She pointed Lofton's nose at the roses he hadn't been smelling. He remembered the most important thing he had learned from Bill Walsh, who coached Stanford his senior season: "You've got to believe you're better than anybody else."

Lofton not only believes that, it's the source of both his calm, unruffled air and his aggressive style. That confidence is what elevates him above ordinary receivers, says Chicago cornerback Leslie Frazier. "He could probably play defensive back because of his competitive nature. He has that edge that a lot of receivers don't have. He wants the ball thrown to him. He wants to get the ball even in the toughest situations." And he usually does.

NEIL LOMAX
HIS FEATHERS WON'T RUFFLE

St. Louis Cardinals
Born February 17, 1959, at Portland, Oregon
Height, 6.03. Weight, 215.

YEAR	CLUB	G	ATT	CMP	PASSING PCT	GAIN	TD	INT	AVG	RUSHING ATT	YDS	AVG	TD
1981	St. Louis NFL	14	236	119	50.4	1575	4	10	6.67	19	104	5.5	2
1982	St. Louis NFL	9	205	109	53.2	1367	5	6	6.67	28	119	4.3	1
1983	St. Louis NFL	13	354	209	59.0	2636	24	11	7.45	27	127	4.7	2
1984	St. Louis NFL	16	560	345	61.6	4614	28	16	8.24	35	184	5.3	3

Neil Lomax was making his first NFL start when the Dallas Cowboy defense coiled up to throw all sorts of doom at him. The safeties were blitzing, and they wanted Lomax to know it. That was how they were going to rattle the rookie.

They thought it might work until Lomax looked across the line of scrimmage, grinned at safety Charlie Waters, and winked. "I really got off on that," Waters said, both amused and impressed.

Hey, this was going to be fun. "Playing the Cowboys was a thrill for me," Lomax said. "Some of the names they have, I grew up hearing them. But I grew up hearing Pat Tilley and Mel Gray and Dan Dierdorf, too, and these guys were my teammates. Of course, there was pressure, but I didn't let it affect me. I just went out and played that game called football. It was the same game I'd been playing in college."

Lomax has given wing to the St. Louis Cardinals' offense ever since 1981, when coach Jim Hanifan turned it over to him 11 games into his rookie year. He has made football fun again in St. Louis, which was the staging ground for Air Coryell in the 1970s but went from 1976 until 1982 without a winning season. In 1984, Lomax was the NFL's fourth-ranked passer and the 9–7 Cardinals had the third-ranked passing game. They came within the last two minutes of the last game of winning the NFC East championship before Washington beat them on a field goal. And they did it because Lomax brought them from a 23–7 halftime deficit to a 27–26 fourth-quarter lead with 25-for-28 passing.

"What Neil Lomax has is a lot of confidence in his ability," Hanifan says. "His confidence radiates to everybody else—to his teammates, to

"I'm not some prima donna who's going to be Joe Cool out there," says Lomax. "I know the game's not going to be centered around me. There are 10 other players who are part of this play. I'm just one of the characters."

anybody else who comes in contact with him. It isn't an arrogance either. He has an innate ability to lead. There's nothing presumptuous or phony about him. He's just him, and the team responds to it."

Players respond to his endearing smile, his contagious enthusiasm, and his Christian peace. Also, to his success. When several Cardinals wanted to meet with Hanifan between the 1983 and 1984 seasons, they insisted on waiting for Lomax to come from his Lake Oswego, Oregon, home, outside Portland.

"I don't think I'm the type who sits back and says, 'I'm the quarterback, I make X amount of money and I'm too cool to be with you guys.' I think the guys know that. They rally around me because they know I'm just like them.

"I'm not some prima donna who's going to be Joe Cool out there. I know the game's not going to be centered around me. There are 10 other players who are part of this play. I'm just one of the characters."

His upbringing was very middle-class suburban, the second of four children whose parents worked for the schools. The athletic genes came from his mother, Carol, a former AAU swimming star. Lomax broke Don Schollander's pool record in a 25-yard race when he was 6, but gave up the sport when he found out about pre-dawn workouts. Baseball was his favorite at Lake Oswego High. He pitched, played first base, and batted .350 over three years. He was going to play college baseball until he met Portland State football coach Darrel (Mouse) Davis in his senior year.

Davis talked Lomax into football and walked him through the sophisticated run-and-shoot passing game, which Davis has made a rage in the USFL. Lomax responded with 90 NCAA Division I-AA records and several for all divisions, including passes for 13,220 yards and 106 touchdowns in four years. As a senior, he passed for 400 yards 12 times. Against Delaware State, he set a record with seven touchdown passes in a quarter. He did it in seven passes. The old record was four. Portland State won 105–0, improving on an earlier 93–7 squeaker.

Scouts called him the next Terry Bradshaw. There were concerns about his college competition, and his style of sprinting out instead of dropping back, but he was 6'3", 214 pounds, strong-armed, and fast. The Cardinals were shocked to be able to draft him in the second round, after 32 other players. Lomax was let down, disappointed. But not bitter. It was time to play.

At the Cardinals' rookie camp, quarterback coach Harry Gilmer told Hanifan, "The kid sees more things than he even needs to look at." Davis had schooled him well in reading defenses, and Lomax had developed an uncanny field sense. In that Dallas game, the second game of the season, Hanifan said the Cowboys surprised him with one blitz, "but he scrambled and had the presence of mind to look downfield. He completed a 62-yard touchdown. Now you *know* the guy can do it."

Lomax was just filling in then because Jim Hart was injured. But 10 games into the 1981 season, Hanifan decided a 37-year-old quarterback was out of place on a young team with a 3–7 record. He decided to sink or swim with Lomax. Hart was bitter, barely speaking to Lomax, and doing nothing to discourage the rift that developed on the team. Some veterans openly supported the popular local hero, the NFL's third-ranked all-time passer. But when Lomax engineered a four-game winning streak, one veteran spoke for the others when he said, "You hate to see it, but the kid's been pretty impressive."

He completed 64 percent of his passes with just two interceptions before St. Louis lost its last two games. In the streak, Lomax threw for two touchdowns and ran for two more. Fans called him the Gateway Gunner. After the third win 27–20 on a hurry-up drive to the winning touchdown pass with 33 seconds left, Lomax said, "I was not a rookie then. I was *the* quarterback."

In the strike-shortened 1982 season, Lomax went 100 straight passes without an interception and finished with six, a league low. He became less cautious the next year, but his interceptions remained rare. His touchdown-to-interception ratio for 1983–84 was 52–27.

St. Louis began 1983 with high hopes off a 5–4 season. But Lomax separated his shoulder in the opener and missed three games. The Cards started 1–5, averaging just 17 points a game. They had to be content with a strong finish, 7–2–1 and

a 27-point average in their last 10 games. Lomax threw for touchdowns in each of the last eight games. A bright future was still at Lomax's fingertips, but it squirmed away every time he reached.

Last year he grabbed it. He had touchdown passes in the first 11 games and was blanked in only one. He cleared 300 yards seven times, 260 in all but three games. His 4,614-yard season was the fourth highest in NFL history. His finale against Washington was an all-timer, 37-for-46 passing for 468 yards, two touchdowns and one interception. He made dumping passes an art wherever a blitzer left an opening, and he was always a deep threat. He played in his first Pro Bowl.

"Neil anticipates," said Roy Green, who led all NFL receivers in yards for 1983–84. "He doesn't give a defensive back that extra moment to see the play develop. If the quarterback anticipates and knows where you're going to be, you have a good chance of making the play."

"What Neil Lomax has is a lot of confidence in his ability," says Cardinal coach Jim Hanifan. "It isn't arrogance, either. He has an innate ability to lead. He's just him, and the team responds to it."

HOWIE LONG
FROM MEAN STREETS TO SWEET DREAMS

Los Angeles Raiders
Born January 6, 1960, at Somerville, Massachusetts
Height, 6.05. Weight, 270.

YEAR	CLUB	G	SACKS
1981	Oakland NFL	16	8½
1982	Los Angeles Raiders NFL	9	5½
1983	Los Angeles Raiders NFL	16	13
1984	Los Angeles Raiders NFL	16	10

Howie Long has seen the ghost of washed-up athletes. He knows what it is to be unknown, unloved, and underfed. He grew up that way in South Boston's mean streets, a beer bottle's throw from the city's notorious Combat Zone. That's why he appreciates his two-Mercedes lifestyle a little more than most pro football players. That's why he is less inclined to take for granted the recent good fortune of two straight all-pro seasons and the 1983 NFL championship as the Los Angeles Raiders' defensive left end.

That's why if his stomach feels the least bit soft at bedtime, Long says he'll hit the floor "for 3,000 situps." Two big seasons? A pittance, says Long. He hasn't played but four. "I've got to go out and do it again. And again. I'm not complacent. I'm neurotic. I worry about whether I'll make it again, whether I'm doing all right, whether I'm working hard enough, whether I'm improving."

"He wants to be great," says Lyle Alzado, Long's kindred spirit and the Raiders' other defensive end. "A lot of athletes today are very spoiled. Howie's not. He's always asking questions, trying to better himself. He's agile, mobile, and hostile. He reminds me of myself at a younger age. He has a lot of inner anger. What'll make him better than the others is, he's from the streets."

So is Alzado, a New Yorker. But where Alzado cultivates the rough image of a man who picks his teeth with a switchblade, Long comes across like the White Shadow. He smiles easily, with a sense of humor that isn't bitter and the intelligence to know the stadium announcer who called him Huey Long had mistaken him for a dead politician.

"I was a human being long before I was a football player," he says, and he makes it sort of a campaign to point out his cohorts' humanity. "We are not let out on the weekends to go to dinner. I don't treat people like poodles just because they're little. Why should people treat me like an ape just because I'm big?"

Off the field, that stereotype is a disconcerting reminder of Long's misspent youth. He had his scraps with thugs and scrapes with the law. "Nothing good ever happened to me until I put a helmet on," he said. But the football field gave him an acceptable place to drain his aggression. He owes more than comfort and fame to that helmet. "It's like legalizing Howie," he says.

Long's size was an advantage in Charlestown, the blue-collar neighborhood where he grew up with his grandmother after his parents divorced when he was 11. The first time he returned from Los Angeles, his car stereo was stolen. Long recalls an economy based on armed robbery, car theft, and shakedowns. "Either you were getting your lunch money taken or you were taking

someone else's," he says. "Going to school was looked down upon. If you went, you got beat up."

Long didn't go. Oh, he started school at four. He was big enough by then. His father was 6'8". But at 13, he was big enough to unload fish crates for $20 a day. All the guys in hs street gang played hooky. "If you didn't hang out, they thought you were a pansy type and you'd get assaulted," Long says. "Every day is a day of survival there. A day of constant peer pressure."

After ninth grade, Long had been in enough fights to get kicked out of the Boston school system. He moved in with his uncle Billy in Milford, a middle-class suburb. Billy imposed a curfew and assigned chores. Long's world turned upside down.

Now it was cool to make good grades, to play sports. He lettered three years in basketball and track. He set district records in the shot put, discus, and javelin that still stand. But he didn't play football until the Milford coach buttonholed him in his junior year. "Football wasn't even a lifetime dream of mine," he says.

He dreamed of college, though. As a high school senior, he missed only three games with a broken ankle. "Sheer fear of not getting a schol-

Cardinal coach Jim Hanifan did a double take the first time he saw Long on film. "I said, 'Who is this guy?' " Now Hanifan calls him "the best defensive end in the game."

Long, who grew up on the mean streets of South Boston, remembers an economy based on armed robbery, car theft, and shakedowns. "Either you were getting your lunch money taken, or you were taking someone else's," he says. "Going to school was looked down upon. If you went, you got beat up."

arship," Long explains. He chose Villanova over some football factories because the coaches promised an education.

Long grew two inches and 55 pounds the summer before he started college. "It was because I got three meals a day, which wasn't a common occurrence for me as a youth," he says. He dominated his competition. Still, it was Villanova. The school gave up football after Long's senior year. The Raiders surprised a lot of people when they drafted him in the second round. "The proudest moment of my life," Long says.

Cardinal coach Jim Hanifan did a double take the first time he saw Long on film. "I said, 'Who is this guy?'" Long's reckless abandon reminded Hanifan of Randy White. Now Hanifan calls him "the best defensive end in the game."

Long led Raider linemen in sacks as a rookie in 1981. But he always has been more than a pass rusher. In the Raiders' 3–4 defense, linemen are assigned to tie up as many blockers as they can so the linebackers can make tackles. "I should show up painted like a duck. I'm a decoy," says Long. Thanks to his notoriety in 1983, his share of blockers usually is three.

"When you draw more of a crowd, it's hard to get the stats," he says. "But when you're drawing a crowd, that's a statistic in itself." So is "holding penalties drawn." Last year, Long counted more than 20.

His sacks tend to come in bunches. A team either commits enough blockers to bury him or it doesn't. In his second pro start, in 1982, Long had three sacks against Kansas City. The next year, when he led the Raiders with 13 sacks, he had three against San Diego and five against Washington. He can only wonder how often he could hang up those numbers if the Raiders always used the four-man lines that make Mark Gastineau so effective. "I'd be embarrassed if I didn't have more than 20 sacks, the way they let him play," Long says.

"There are guys who are bigger, guys who are stronger, guys who are faster, and guys who are meaner," Raider linebacker Matt Millen says. "But none of them puts it together the way he does. He does everything."

And plays every position on the line. "They can play me at cornerback if they want," Long says. As coach Tom Flores says, "Howie just loves to play." Just playing is better than being voted the NFL's second best defensive player, as he was in 1983. It's even better than wearing a Super Bowl ring. "There's nothing like the chase," Long says. "Nothing. I'm not big on trophies. I'm big on participating."

He isn't above reflecting, though. When Long's gang was showering in fire hydrants, his wife, Diane, was using lace napkins at the swim club. Imagine that. She was runner-up for Miss New Jersey in 1978. "Until I went to her mother's house," Long says, "I didn't know you could get peaches any way except in a can." Now he could buy a peach tree.

"Most of my friends are either dead or in jail," Long says. "There were a lot of tragedies. But this is a party for me. Getting paid to play football and to wear a certain brand of shoe. I never would have dreamed. As a kid, my goal was survival. So this is all a fantasyland. It's the greatest feeling in the world to know you've made it."

RONNIE LOTT
CATALYST FOR A CHAMPION

San Francisco 49ers
Born May 8, 1959, at Albuquerque, New Mexico
Height, 6.00. Weight, 199.

YEAR	CLUB	G	INTERCEPTIONS			
			NO	YDS	AVG	TD
1981	San Francisco NFL	16	7	117	16.7	3
1982	San Francisco NFL	9	2	95	47.5	1
1983	San Francisco NFL	15	4	22	5.5	0
1984	San Francisco NFL	12	4	26	6.5	0

To Ronnie Lott, it's just a small detail that his unit has to begin each play without the ball. "He plays defense like it's offense," legendary halfback O. J. Simpson says. He attacks. He fights for the ball. He even scores.

Lott returned three interceptions for touchdowns as a rookie cornerback in 1981, and he did it once more in the playoffs. "He makes things happen," says San Francisco coach Bill Walsh, and for the 49ers, they're nearly always good things.

Even as a rookie, Lott was being called the new kind of prototype cornerback. His aggressive magnetism for the ball was the ideal antidote to modern offenses that score so swiftly. Miami coach Don Shula says, "The thing you have to do on defense now is take the ball away." Lott forces turnovers, he covers receivers man-to-man, and he scatters bruises in his wake. Doing all those things, Lott and fellow corner Eric Wright helped shut down the NFL's all-time best passing offense in San Francisco's 38–16 Super Bowl victory over Miami last January.

"They say he isn't fast enough," Chicago coach Mike Ditka says, "but he's fast enough to stay with receivers. The thing I like about him is the way he sticks his nose in it. He takes no prisoners."

Walsh calls Lott "probably the most physical" defensive back in the league. "He's such a great athlete, he could probably play all four spots in the secondary," Walsh says. "He could also play on offense as a running back or wide receiver, and he'd be an asset there, too."

"I like the way he sticks his nose in it," says Mike Ditka. "He takes no prisoners."

Lott actually started different games at wide receiver, quarterback, and safety as a senior at Eisenhower High School in Rialto, California, near Los Angeles. With the 49ers, Lott has played both strong and free safety, and Walsh has considered making him a free safety permanently. That would give him more freedom in gravitating toward the ball, the reason he played strong safety at Southern California. Lott led the 49ers in tackles in 1983, something cornerbacks simply don't do. He was 30 ahead of the runner-up. "He's the best run defender of any defensive back in the league," says Ram coach John Robinson, who coached Lott at USC.

The move to cornerback was not easy. But just as strong safety was the key position in college secondary, the hot spot in the pros is left corner. That's where the 49ers wanted their best defensive back. "I hope my eagerness will help me overcome my mistakes," said Lott, who insisted he was not a natural. "You can't get a big head, because someone in this league will make it little real fast."

Lott joined a 49er team that had gone 2–14, 2–14, and 6–10 in the previous three years, and the secondary was clearly its weakness. The 49ers had tried out 32 defensive backs two years earlier, in 1979. Their 1980 opponents had completed 66.1 percent of their passes, the highest in league history.

So Walsh not only made Lott the eighth choice in the 1981 draft, he added Wright and strong safety Carlton Williamson with his next picks. He planned to start all three. "A calculated risk," Walsh said of starting three rookie defensive backs. "Terrifying," said Carl Peterson, then the Eagles' personnel director.

People laughed when Walsh called the secondary San Francisco's strength before the season began. They didn't *play* like rookies. They weren't hesitant. After their first exhibition, Walsh said, "They went out and played like they had played in college. They didn't even think about whether it was professional ball or not."

"They're young, but they know how to go after the ball better than anybody," said Woody Widenhofer, Pittsburgh's defensive coordinator. "Especially Ronnie Lott."

Lott couldn't understand the fuss. Of course, he went for the ball. Wasn't that the object of the game? "I think it's such a waste to just bring a guy down when you can do so much more," Lott said. The 49er defensive backs even spent part of their pregame warmups tackling each other, trying to knock the ball loose.

The 49ers had the NFL's best record that season, 13–3. But still, people had trouble taking them seriously. Three rookie defensive backs? The respect didn't start coming until they beat Cincinnati in the Super Bowl.

"Our defense was what did it," guard John Ayers said of the 1981 season. The 49ers scored 21 points or less in seven of their last nine victories, 17 or less in four victories.

Adding the rookie defensive backs, linebacker Jack Reynolds and defensive end Fred Dean, the 49ers made remarkable one-year improvement. They went from twenty-seventh to second in total yards allowed, twenty-seventh to third in passing yield. They allowed only a 53.1 percent completion rate, the NFL's sixth lowest. Their interceptions improved from 17 to 27, fifth best, and their touchdown passes dropped from 29 to 16, tied for sixth. After allowing 415 points in 1980, they gave up just 250 in 1981, second fewest in the league.

Lott scored more touchdowns than he gave up. He ranked second to Reynolds in tackles. He was consensus all-pro and probably would have been Rookie of the Year if he hadn't broken in at the same time as Lawrence Taylor.

The 49ers backslid to 3–6 in 1982, when some teammates' overgrown heads and drug problems were the residue of sudden success. When they rebounded to 10–6, Lott was the 1983 NFL Alumni Association's Defensive Back of the Year, and all-pro again. His 1984 season began with an ankle injury on the third play; he missed four games with that and a dislocated shoulder and played a few at free safety. But he made one all-pro team and his fourth Pro Bowl. He remained the defensive heart and soul of the NFL's first 15-game winner and 1984 champion.

"He's a guy who comes along once every five or six years," says Dick Steinberg, New England's personnel director. "He's a catalyst type guy who can make other people play better. He's got so much athletic ability and competitiveness that he's going to make plays all over the field."

Lott was athletic enough to letter on USC's basketball team as a junior. In football, he was voted both Most Valuable Player and Most Inspirational as a senior. "At SC, I don't think I've ever seen a defensive player better than Ronnie," Robinson says.

What's more, he graduated in four years while USC was weathering academic scandal. He finished in summer school while working at a steel mill during the day. "You can only do it if you make it your priority," Lott said. "More football players would graduate if they could see how vital it is. That's surprisingly hard for an athlete to grasp."

But Lott always has made the unusual look routine. On the football field, he does what's expected and goes one step further.

"He'll get himself in position *and* make the play," 49er defensive coordinator George Seifert says. "A lot of guys get in position and figure they've done their job. Then the play gets away from them. But that's when he accelerates, right at the critical moment."

"It's a waste to bring a guy down when you can do so much more," Lott said of his love for turnovers. The 49er defensive backs even practice tackling each other, trying to knock the ball loose.

DAN MARINO
WHIZ KID WIZARD

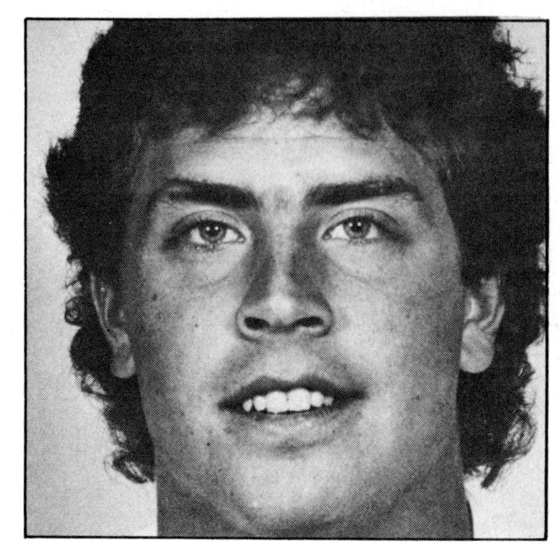

Miami Dolphins
Born September 15, 1961, at Pittsburgh, Pennsylvania
Height, 6.03. Weight, 214.

YEAR	CLUB	G	ATT	CMP	PASSING PCT	GAIN	TD	INT	AVG	RUSHING ATT	YDS	AVG	TD
1983	Miami NFL	11	296	173	58.4	2210	20	6	7.47	28	45	1.6	2
1984	Miami NFL	16	564	362	64.2	5084	48	17	9.01	28	-7	-0.3	0

For all the raving about the cannon in Dan Marino's right arm, there is an even bigger reason he has been all but canonized after two NFL seasons. "He's a winner because he's not afraid to do the things you have to do to win," says Don Shula, Marino's Miami Dolphins coach. "He attacks it. He meets it head on."

He sends the ball downfield aggressively, daring defenses to stop him. He's not reckless about it, even though he often throws to covered receivers, because as Pittsburgh safety Donnie Shell says, "His throws leave you no reasonable reaction time." Just like other quarterbacks, Marino takes what the defense gives him. But in his case, that's practically anything he wants.

In an average game last season, he passed for 317 yards, 3 touchdowns, and 1 interception. He threw for touchdowns three fewer times than the Dolphins punted. He set league records for touchdowns, completions, and yards, and he *doubled* the team records. His four 400-yard games, another record, were one short of the career record, which took Sonny Jurgensen 19 years. Yet despite his downfield daring, Marino never threw more interceptions than touchdown passes until San Francisco stymied Miami in the Super Bowl.

"Kind of makes you wonder what he'll be like when he's 27, doesn't it?" Dolphin guard Ed Newman said.

"He's the best quarterback I ever saw," said Terry Bradshaw, one of the best. "I've never meant anything more in my life. He passed me a long time ago."

Marino's hand was barely big enough to grip a ball when his father, Dan Sr., taught him the Joe Namath–style release, flicking the wrist without bringing the ball back past the ear. He doesn't pass the ball so much as he launches it. "He's like

"He's the best quarterback I ever saw," said Terry Bradshaw, one of the best. "I've never meant anything more in my life. He passed me a long time ago."

a gun that's already cocked," 49er safety Carlton Williamson says. Shula calls Marino's arm "the quickest I've ever seen." That lets him hold the ball longer, giving receivers more time to get open. It also is why, despite substandard speed, he has been sacked just 27 times after 31 pro games and 1,001 passes.

Blitzing doesn't help. The Steelers were dominating the AFC championship game, ahead 14–10 when Miami got the ball 2:43 before halftime. Within two minutes, Miami led 24–14. Marino passed for playoff records of 421 yards and four touchdowns.

"He's never indecisive," Shula says. Marino speed-reads a defense and picks out his receiver in the time it takes to drop back. He can loft the ball if he has to. "You know if you get open, the ball will be there on time and in a spot where you can catch it."

As a rookie, Marino sometimes did react too slowly to overloaded defenses. But he would come back to the huddle and say it was his fault. "You hear that, you go crazy," Newman says.

"Hey, this guy is a self-correcting machine."

One reason veterans haven't minded his coming down on them is that he does it to himself. After a touchdown pass, he runs to the receiver and hugs him. "He really is one of the guys," Newman says. "Some other quarterbacks have such elite postures. But he is cussing and getting down in the mud with the rest of us."

Off the field, the Namath comparisons break down. Marino calls himself boring. Others call him smug and coarse. He's been said to strut standing still. That's the flip side of his boundless confidence, which makes him unafraid to fail. Perhaps he admits mistakes so easily because he knows he can correct them easily.

In his first NFL start, after losing two interceptions and two fumbles in the first quarter, he said, "Don't worry, we've got this game in the bag." The players loved it. "You never see Dan hang his head after he throws an interception," Shula says. "He'll come off the field and ask, 'OK, what did I do wrong?' Nothing seems to bother him or upset him. I think going through that senior year at Pittsburgh helped mature him."

That was when the hometown fans' cheers turned to boos in his senior college season. He had led Pitt to three 11–1 seasons. As a junior, he finished fourth in Heisman voting after throwing for 34 touchdowns and 23 interceptions. But his senior year, Pitt went 9–3. The touchdowns and interceptions were 17 and 23. Drug rumors were so pervasive, he took tests to silence them.

His scouting reports soured. He was the 27th player drafted, the 6th quarterback. But the problem in his senior year had been a bad *team*. Marino was the MVP of two post-season all-star games. "I saw how fast things can change," he says. "In this business it's best to stay on an even keel."

Marino went to Central Catholic High School and Pitt within blocks of his home in Pittsburgh's integrated, blue-collar Oakland section. He says his biggest athletic influence was his father, a newspaper truck driver. He's a homebody. His shoe endorsement contract calls for three pairs to children of unemployed steelworkers for every touchdown run or pass.

"Everyone asks about the pressure," Marino says. "But I don't think about that. My father once said, 'Pressure is having six kids, half of them sick, and you've been laid off at the mill.' This isn't pressure."

The Dolphins were perfect for him. They had an excellent offensive line, good receivers, and a brilliant coach, flexible enough to accommodate

In Marino's first NFL start, after losing two interceptions and two fumbles in the first quarter, he said, "Don't worry, we've got this game in the bag." The players loved it.

him. They also had enough problems to bring out the best in him.

Marino was not only Miami's offense last year, he was their defense. He took the run away from opponents. Until the Super Bowl, he covered up the absence of a running game. His staggering numbers may not rise with his own improvement because future Dolphin teams may not need them. But when they did need them, Marino produced. The Super Bowl was billed as the excellent team against the excellent quarterback, and reasonable people picked the quarterback. No one team was bigger than this man.

"He's an anomaly. A freak," Newman said. "I kept saying, 'It's going to go away. He'll go back to the standards of a normal quarterback.' But it didn't. Five, six, seven weeks. Maybe he's for real. I had to pinch myself. He just thinks he can get it done any time against anyone, and it's catching. There's electricity in the huddle."

In his first league game, the third in 1983, Marino threw touchdown passes on his first two drives. He won the starting job for the sixth game and became the first rookie to lead a conference in passing. He was elected to start the Pro Bowl. The Dolphins averaged 15.6 points in 1983 before Marino started, 27 in his starts.

People said it was unfair to expect steady improvement. The Dolphins averaged 32 last year. Under Marino, they're 21–4 and 2–2 in playoff games. In 31 NFL appearances, he has passed for 5,170 yards, 77 touchdowns, and 30 interceptions, and he's still rising. He threw four touchdown passes in each of his last four league games, averaged 361 yards in his last six.

"I don't look on it as being difficult," Marino says. "I look at it as a chance to go out and do something fun. The chance to be a professional quarterback is something that doesn't happen to too many people." It seems Marino has everyone in awe except Marino.

ART MONK
MONEY IN THE BANK

Washington Redskins
Born December 5, 1957, at White Plains, New York
Height, 6.03. Weight, 209.

YEAR	CLUB	G	RUSHING				PASS RECEIVING			
			ATT	YDS	AVG	TD	NO	YDS	AVG	TD
1980	Washington NFL	16	-	-	-	-	58	797	13.7	3
1981	Washington NFL	16	1	-5	-5.0	0	56	894	16.0	6
1982	Washington NFL	9	7	21	3.0	0	35	447	12.8	1
1983	Washington NFL	12	3	-19	-6.3	0	47	746	15.9	5
1984	Washington NFL	16	2	18	9.0	0	106	1372	12.9	7

Art Monk tends to get lost in the crowd, but he usually emerges from it with the football. For four years, he had done the Redskin receivers' dirty work, bouncing off linebackers over the middle to make the tough catches that keep first-down chains moving. He was easy to take for granted. Redskin players called him Money because he made so many clutch catches, but the real money went to the glamor guys on the outside lane, making touchdown catches and dancing in the end zone.

His teammates were the only ones who appreciated Monk until desperation forced the Redskins to make him the top single-season receiver in NFL history.

Monk's 106 catches in 1984 broke a 23-year-old record. Charley Hennigan had caught 101 in two fewer games but had done it against early AFL defensive backs, who appeared to be bartenders and cab drivers hastily fitted for shoulder pads. Monk caught 64 more than the Redskins' runner-up, only two fewer than their next *four* receivers. He even had a fan section in RFK Stadium called the Art Gallery. It might not have happened without the injury to Charlie Brown, Washington's more heralded wideout. But when the Redskins had to turn to Monk for extra help, he didn't leave them empty-handed. "I've always thought I was capable of doing this," he said. "It was just a matter of getting the chance."

"If they throw to him 100 times, he'll catch all 100 of them," Colt cornerback Eugene Daniel said. "He makes catches that almost seem impossible." But Monk would not pose for any legend-builders. "I'm not the star on the top of the tree," he said. "I'm more like the bulb, one of the ornaments." He was sounding like all those people who had overlooked him.

Monk was worried before the Redskins' last game, when he needed seven catches to break the record. "I was almost scared that I was not going to do it," he recalled. "I was saying, 'What will people think if I don't? What if I get in there and I'm a nervous wreck?' "

What if he drops an easy touchdown pass? Darned if that didn't happen. "The first time I have ever seen him drop a long pass," coach Joe Gibbs said. But before long, Monk lost track of the record, which he broke almost incidentally with a 36-yard catch midway through the third quarter. The Redskins needed to beat St. Louis to win the NFC East. They would need all 11 of Monk's catches, and both of his touchdowns. They trailed St. Louis in the last two minutes,

third-and-19 on the Cardinal 47, when Monk made his 106th catch. He had to dive past the first-down stick. The play, so typical, set up the winning field goal four downs later.

As important as the record was, Monk said after the game, "More than anything, I'd like to win the Super Bowl." The thought had consumed him ever since he missed the Redskins' championship run two years earlier because he broke his foot in the last regular season game. Before then, he had never had to miss even a practice. "It was like being rich all your life and suddenly being poor," Monk said.

The Redskins had expected a lot from Monk when they picked him 18th in the 1980 draft, ending 11 years without a first-round choice. Before draft day ended, they traded their leading receiver from 1979. They compared him to ex-Redskin Charley Taylor, the NFL's all-time leading receiver before Charlie Joiner broke his rec-

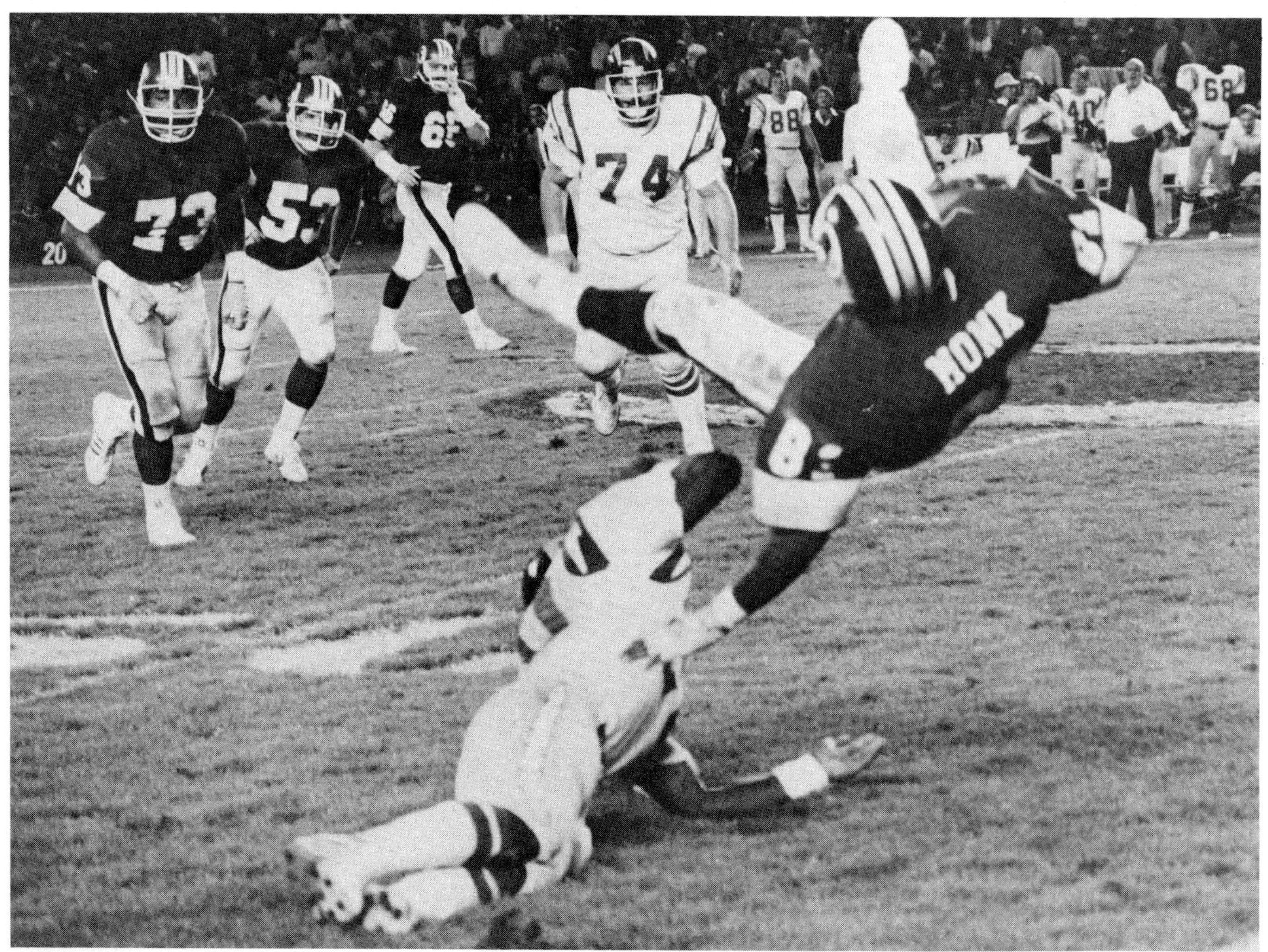

Monk, who is perfectly content to be away from football's spotlight, said "If you start talking about yourself, you get away from what you're supposed to be doing. Once you start thinking, 'Hey, I'm good,' you get your block knocked off."

ord last year. Like Taylor, Monk had been a running back, averaging 4.5 yards a carry as a sophomore and junior at Syracuse. He was the Orangemen's leading all-time receiver.

But all this attention surprised him. Monk didn't expect to be a pro player, let alone a first-round pick. He was planning to use his degree in an advertising career.

Looking back through 1984 to his first four seasons, Monk said, "I had a lot to prove because I really hadn't been able to do much." He hadn't been a disappointment. Coaches stopped whispering after his first training camp that he couldn't play. "I think I've been a pretty steady guy," Monk said. "I've been there when they've needed me." But still. He was a receiver with good speed and exceptional size, 6'3" and 209 pounds, the man Gibbs calls, "probably the strongest receiver I've ever been around." And he hadn't caught 58 balls since his rookie year. Something was missing. Where was the flash?

"I think the thing that Art has on other receivers," Brown said, "is that he's a good inside and a good outside receiver." The inside ones are harder to find. By doing the work usually required of tight ends, Monk helped the Redskins' running game. They could use better blockers at tight end.

Sure, it's scary over the middle, Monk admits. "Any receiver who says no, I think, is telling a lie. I won't say I don't like to do it. But there's always something in the back of my mind that one of those times I go in, I might not come out."

Monk seems too soft-spoken and thoughtful to be a pro athlete.

He says, "I sometimes get the impression that people don't think I'm bright because I'm quiet." He doesn't curse. He didn't spike the ball after touchdowns until some kids told him he was boring. He had to be talked into joining the Fun Bunch celebrations of Redskin receivers. He's not the sort to send up flares just to get noticed. "Some athletes on other teams I've gotten to meet, they're so cocky and arrogant," Monk says. "They're always bragging on how well they do this and that. That just turns me off."

He's an athlete, though. When he was all-state in high school track and football, he seriously considered becoming a decathlete. But he also liked art and music in high school. His father's cousin was jazz pianist Thelonious Monk. Growing up in the New York suburb of White Plains, he recalls, "Athletics wasn't a very big thing in my family. We never went to many games." Even now, Monk says, "I don't want a life where it's football, football, football."

He would have been just as happy without the spotlight from the record. Interviews made him uncomfortable. "If you start talking about yourself, you get away from what you're supposed to be doing," he said. "Once you start thinking, 'Hey, I'm good,' you get your block knocked off."

The record crept up subtly. Through 11 games, Monk was well below a record pace with 63 catches, tops in the league but only seven ahead of No. 5. The hubbub didn't start until he caught 13 in week 11. Now he had 82, and his 6.3-catch pace would get him to 101. The comparisons with Taylor resurfaced. "I'm just happy to be able to work with him," said Taylor, now Washington's receiver coach.

Even as the new sensation, Monk was more steady than striking. He caught at least eight passes six times, fewer than five only three times. He finished the season with 10 catches in the Redskins' playoff loss. He even made the game-ending tackle after an interception. As Gibbs said, "When things weren't going good for us this year, Art Monk was there. When things are going good for us, Art Monk is still there."

The top single-season receiver in history (106 catches), Monk never spiked the ball until some kids told him he was boring.

JOE MONTANA
DR. COOL

San Francisco 49ers
Born June 11, 1956, at Monongahela, Pennsylvania
Height, 6.02. Weight, 195.

| | | | **PASSING** | | | | | | | | **RUSHING** | | | |
YEAR	CLUB	G	ATT	CMP	PCT	GAIN	TD	INT	AVG	ATT	YDS	AVG	TD
1979	San Francisco NFL	16	23	13	56.5	96	1	0	4.17	3	22	7.3	0
1980	San Francisco NFL	15	273	176	64.5	1795	15	9	6.58	32	77	2.4	2
1981	San Francisco NFL	16	488	311	63.7	3565	19	12	7.31	25	95	3.8	2
1982	San Francisco NFL	9	346	213	61.6	2613	17	11	7.55	30	118	3.9	1
1983	San Francisco NFL	16	515	332	64.5	3910	26	12	7.59	61	284	4.7	2
1984	San Francisco NFL	16	432	279	64.6	3630	28	10	8.4	39	118	3.0	2

He was the Comeback Kid in college. Now he's the man who makes big plays on the run. You'd think Joe Montana just goes out on the field with an uncluttered mind and pulls game-winning passes out of his helmet. But the key to Montana's spontaneity is his preparation. "You try to think of everything before the snap," he says, "because after the snap, it's just reactions."

That's hardly the swashbuckling behavior people expect of someone who Notre Dame fans said saved more lost causes than St. Jude. Montana isn't flamboyant. He doesn't even swagger. He almost looks bored. But those bedroom eyes aren't glazing over, they're concentrating. Montana can't afford the luxury of bubbling emo-

tions. He is very precise about the way he matter-of-factly slices defenses to ribbons.

"Pressure is more a challenge than anything else," Montana says. "It's when everything else is on the line and it becomes you against your opponent. Maybe that is how I cope with it. I make myself forget about it and zero in on what you have to do. So it is no longer pressure. It is just a job with a series of things that must be done. You concentrate on those things."

He has done it well enough to be the MVP in both the San Francisco 49ers' Super Bowl victories, for 1981 and 1984. For six NFL seasons, he is the highest rated passer in NFL history. Last year, when he led the NFC in passing, he improved his

career records for the highest completion percentage and the lowest interception percentage.
He has thrown for nearly twice as many touchdowns as interceptions. But darn it, he sure
would like to cut down on those interceptions.

Montana is such an unimposing physical specimen that when 49er wide receiver Dwight Clark
first saw him at camp, he wondered who the
kicker was. "I thought, 'Man, that can't be Joe
Montana,' " Clark says. He had seen Montana beat
his Clemson team with two fourth-quarter touchdown passes. He had heard about the three
fourth-quarter comebacks—from 14, 20, and 10
points behind—even before Montana won the
starting job as a junior and led Notre Dame to the
1977 national championship. Montana won the
job after directing the Irish to 17 points in 16
minutes against Purdue. When he took off his
warm-up jacket, his teammates started celebrating as if they were winning, not down by 10.

"When he's in the game, you always feel like
you've got a shot," said Ken McAfee, then an Irish
tight end. "You look in Joe's eyes and you know
he's not giving up, so you don't either."

NFL scouts were unimpressed. They questioned his consistency and his arm strength. Bill
Walsh, the 49er coach who drafted him in the
third round, said, "There are many people in pro
football who get hung up on size and strength for
quarterbacks. But there's much more to being a
quarterback than having a strong arm."

The best thing Montana does is make something out of nothing. "When things start breaking
down, he's got the ability to move and see everything that's happening around him," Redskin
quarterback Joe Theismann says. Where Miami's
Dan Marino has the rifle arm to throw before the
pass rushers get to him, Montana doesn't let them
get to him until he throws. After last season's
Super Bowl, Miami nose tackle Bob Baumhower
said trying to catch Montana "was like chasing a
rabbit."

The game was a prime example of Montana at
his surgical best. He carved Miami's defense for a
Super Bowl record 331 yards, three touchdowns,
and nearly a 70 percent completion rate. He left
the pocket to throw, he ran for first downs, he
found open receivers and he hit them on stride.
"Joe thinks on the run better than anyone I've
ever seen," Clark says. "He loves to scramble
around and make something up and pull it out."

But he can only do it because he is so aware of
where his receivers are going, how they'll adjust
to the defense. San Francisco uses a precise, ball-
control passing offense that can't afford to waste

**After last season's Super Bowl, Miami nose
tackle Bob Baumhower said trying to catch
Montana was "like chasing a rabbit."**

a down. Montana is not only thorough about
studying that offense and opponents' defenses, he
is just as persnickety about little things like his
dropback, getting the right weight distribution,
and foot placement. Those are the reasons Clark
says, "You never see him throw the ball into
coverage."

"The ball always seems to get to the receiver a
half-second early," says Guy Benjamin, his back-
up man. "So many times, a quarterback will get it
there a half-second late—and it gets broken up.
Joe seems to be aware of exactly how much time
he has."

He is an all-around athlete, despite appearances. He pitched perfect games and batted .500
in Little League. He high jumped 6'9" when he
was 15. North Carolina State offered him a scholarship for basketball, where he played every position. But football is king in Monongahela, Pennsylvania, the steel town where Montana grew up.
His boyhood idol, Joe Namath, grew up 30 miles
away. He dreamed of playing for Notre Dame.

Montana capped his comeback legend in his
final Cotton Bowl. The Irish trailed 34–12 while

"I approach Sunday just like a Space Invaders game," Montana says. "I just try to be relaxed, to stay loose. I laugh."

Montana battled illness in the locker room from halftime until 7½ minutes remained. It was enough time to throw for three touchdowns and two two-point conversions, the last pair with no time left, to beat Houston 35–34. "It's not that I had any mystical power. I never stepped back and said, 'Wow this is Gipper material.' I was just out there, trying to win." And as Clark says, "He hates to lose at anything, even dominoes."

"I approach Sunday just like a Space Invaders game," Montana says. "I just try to be relaxed, to stay loose. I laugh."

It's only pressure if he can't control it. Pressure is attracting a mob whenever he leaves the house. It's bad enough at restaurants, but Montana says people sit outside his house in cars, waiting and staring. While his composure has made him famous, fame is the only thing that tests his composure.

That may be why he's on his third marriage. He would rather live a low-profile life. He thinks of himself as a guy who forgets grocery lists and hits his thumb with a hammer, not a celebrity. Acquaintances agree he's genuinely nice, although he's standoffish even with teammates. "More than friendship, you want their respect," he says.

He got it dramatically in his fifth NFL start, in 1980. He engineered the biggest comeback in NFL history, wiping out New Orleans' 35–7 halftime lead to win 38–35 in overtime. The 49ers won the 1981 NFC championship by driving 89 yards in the last 5 minutes, scoring on Montana's famous pass to Clark with 51 seconds left. He overcame a 21–0 deficit in the 1983 championship game with three fourth-quarter touchdown passes before Washington won 24–21.

Last year was Montana's best season, Walsh said, because he could see more of the field. The 49ers no longer limited their passing offense to half the field. But even in 1981, Walsh said, "It's hard to believe this is only his third season. He has the poise, the command of a 10-year veteran." Emotions have always been something he only stirred in others. Montana himself is as cool as the blade of a scalpel.

WARREN MOON
THE LONG ROAD TO SUCCESS

Houston Oilers
Born November 18, 1956, at Los Angeles, California
Height, 6.03. Weight, 210.

YEAR	CLUB	G	ATT	CMP	PCT	GAIN	TD	INT	AVG	ATT	YDS	AVG	TD
					PASSING						**RUSHING**		
1978	Edmonton CFL	15	173	89	51.4	1112	5	7	6.43	30	114	3.8	1
1979	Edmonton CFL	16	274	149	54.4	2382	20	12	8.69	56	150	2.7	2
1980	Edmonton CFL	16	331	181	54.7	3127	25	11	9.45	55	352	6.4	3
1981	Edmonton CFL	15	378	237	62.7	3959	27	12	1047	50	298	6.0	3
1982	Edmonton CFL	16	562	333	59.3	5000	36	16	8.90	54	259	4.8	4
1983	Edmonton CFL	16	664	380	57.2	5648	31	19	8.51	85	527	6.2	3
1984	Houston NFL	16	450	259	57.6	3338	12	14	7.42	58	211	3.6	1

At long last, Warren Moon was wanted. Half a dozen NFL teams were stumbling over each other for the privilege of making him financially secure for the rest of his life. He was a freak of football nature, a proven winning quarterback in the prime of his career who was an absolutely free agent, as free to choose his employer as an accountant or an engineer. That freedom touched off the NFL's biggest recruiting war since it's merger with the AFL. When Moon made his decision February 3, 1984, Houston Oiler executives broke open the champagne.

Moon was a free agent in the first place because he hadn't been drafted. He had been the Pacific Eight Conference Player of the Year in 1977. He led Washington to a 27–20 Rose Bowl victory over Michigan and was the game's Most Valuable Player. His credentials seemed to be in order. But scouts couldn't seem to help themselves from turning a black quarterback's running ability into a demerit. They also estimated Moon's height at two inches shorter than his listed 6'3". He figured to be a late draft choice before he signed with Edmonton of the Canadian League, so after that, he was overlooked completely.

The same thing had happened after Moon graduated from Hamilton High School in West Los Angeles. He had been a high school All-American, but he didn't have to fend off a mob of recruiters eager to make him a big-time college quarter-back. He didn't have to fend off anybody. He went to West Los Angeles Junior College for a year before Washington coach Don James took a chance on him. Even at Washington, he heard so many boos his first year and a half that he said he almost transferred.

"I've had to prove myself my whole life," Moon said after signing with the Oilers. "But I'm kind of glad. I can look back and say nothing has been handed to me."

Moon grew up in West Los Angeles with six sisters and a widowed mother who taught him the basics in shifting for himself. He learned to cook, to sew. He tinkered with recipes. Eventually, he settled on seven recipes for chocolate chip cookies that became so popular, W. Moon's Chocolate Chippery had several outlets in Edmonton and expanded to Houston. In everything Moon did, he learned to be thorough.

That's why he went on such a drawn out tour of prospective employers when he jumped from the CFL to the NFL. Part of it was to let the coaches and owners know him better, so they would part more willingly with more money. But it was just as important for Moon to get to know *them* better, so he could make an educated decision. He truly agonized over it.

"Warren is 27 going on 58," his agent, Leigh Steinberg, says of his deliberate thought processes. In deciding to hire Steinberg, Moon had to meet with him more than 20 times. That was just for an agent. Now he was shopping for his future.

"I've always tried to put things in perspective." Moon says. "I do things one step at a time."

He visited the Giants, Eagles, Buccaneers, Raiders, Saints, Seahawks, Oilers, and the USFL's New Jersey Generals. The decision came down to Seattle, where he had played college ball, and Houston, which had just hired his Edmonton coach, Hugh Campbell. Houston had other advantages. It was a bigger city. The team was young and in desperate need of a quarterback. It had gone 3–22 the previous two years. Aside from a starting job, clearly nothing would be handed to Moon in 1984, but the horizon was broad with promise. Besides, the Oilers offered more money, $6 million for five years.

"I'd be lying if I said I wasn't thinking about the money," Moon said. Still, there were more important pots at the end of his cross-country rainbow. The money made him uncomfortable, especially when his ride to the Giants' office took him past street people using a garbage can for their furnace and stove.

"I'm looking for exposure," Moon said. "I played six years in a league where nobody in the NFL knew who I was."

Oh, word filtered down. Even NFL people tend to notice their poor northern cousin when the same team wins five straight Grey Cups, as Moon's Eskimos did with CFL championships in 1978–82. They were 78–23–5 in Moon's six regular seasons, six games better than the NFL's best team, Dallas, in that stretch.

Moon became a regular late in his second season, 1979, and was the Outstanding Offensive Player in two of his last three Grey Cup games. He won his first regular-season MVP award in 1983, when he set a pro football record with 5,648 yards passing and led Edmonton in rushing with 527 yards. In one game against Montreal, Moon passed for 555 yards and five touchdowns. He had at least 5,000 yards and 30 touchdown passes in both 1982 and 1983. "It just wasn't the same challenge anymore," Moon said. "I needed something new."

It would take some adjusting to play in the NFL. Canadian fields are 10 yards longer and $11\frac{2}{3}$ wider. Canadian rules permit 12 players per team and three downs, not four. The more wide open game demands quarterbacks with a strong arm and quick feet. But they don't have to be as intelligent or as disciplined as NFL quarterbacks, who face better defensive backs and more varied and sophisticated pass coverage schemes. Moon would have to learn to stay in the pass pocket, solve the coverage puzzle, and take advantage of its weakness.

The last star Canadian quarterback to try the NFL, former Notre Damer Tom Clements, had gone back north after one season on Kansas City's bench. Redskin quarterback Joe Theismann starred for Toronto in three CFL seasons, but he was in his third NFL season before he played regularly and his sixth before he played particularly well. Houston needed to have Moon ready yesterday, if not sooner.

Moon was not a typical Canadian sprint-out passer. He had the mechanics for dropping back and firing the ball quickly. His arm was a cannon, and an accurate one. He didn't just throw for high completion percentages and low interceptions. He let receivers make catches without breaking stride. "I didn't have to dive for anything," said Butch Johnson, an Oiler receiver during Moon's first practice. "The ball was always right in my chest. It's a receiver's dream."

The Oilers lost their first ten games, but they won three of their last six. Moon made the all-rookie teams. He completed 63.1 percent of his passes in those last six games. He threw only 14 interceptions all year, with the league's seventh lowest percentage.

Campbell projected him as "a real superstar in the NFL. He has the leadership qualities, intellectual ability, pure passing talent, ability to pass on the run, and above all, a great competitive instinct."

Above even that is Moon's intangible aura, the blend of wisdom and quiet confidence that prompts Steinberg to call him Yoda. To illustrate Moon's leadership, Steinberg says he has lost count of all the teammates Moon has sent him as clients. "He's got that rare quality," Steinberg says, "to make people comfortable following him anywhere. They know he won't lead them astray."

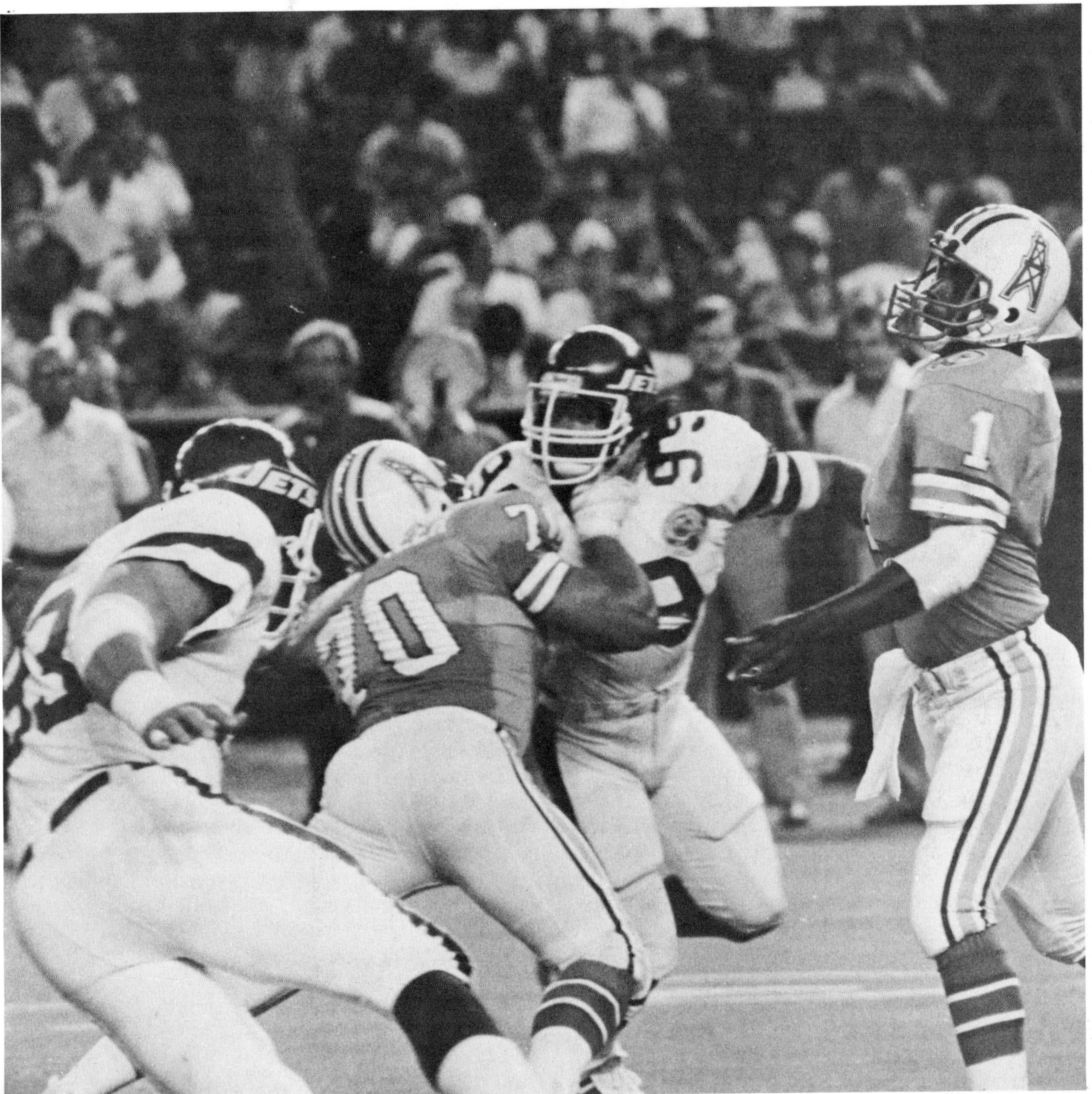

"I've had to prove myself my whole life," Moon said after signing with the Oilers. "But I'm kind of glad. I can look back and say nothing has been handed to me."

ANTHONY MUÑOZ
PILLAR OF STRENGTH

Cincinnati Bengals
Born August 19, 1958, at Ontario, California
Height, 6.06. Weight, 278.

YEAR	CLUB	G
1980	Cincinnati NFL	16
1981	Cincinnati NFL	16
1982	Cincinnati NFL	9
1983	Cincinnati NFL	16
1984	Cincinnati NFL	16

If Anthony Munoz had been any less spectacular, the scouts would have cut him off at the knees. Scouts like their high draft choices to be low on risks. They don't like to see knees that look like railroad yards from surgical scars. When they looked at Munoz, they saw souvenirs from two operations on his right knee and one on his left. They saw nearly 300 pounds those knees would have to support. They saw the distinct possibility of a three-year career. But when they looked past Munoz's medical chart, everything they saw made them blink.

Forrest Gregg remembers scouting Munoz at Southern Cal before the 1980 draft. He was Cincinnati's coach at the time, a Hall-of-Fame offensive lineman who still looked like a mean match for a blocking sled. Gregg told Munoz to get into his stance at offensive tackle, and Gregg was going to pass rush against him. "He put one arm out and knocked me flat," Gregg recalled. "When he did that, I said, 'We've got to have this guy.' "

The Bengals made Munoz the third choice in that draft. If they hadn't taken the gamble, the next team would have. "He's one of the greatest players at any position I ever saw," said John Robinson, Munoz's college coach who had been a Raider assistant.

It took him three days of training camp to win the Bengals' starting job at left tackle. He made the Pro Bowl in his second season, and hasn't missed one since. For his second season, when the Bengals went to the Super Bowl, Munoz was named Offensive Lineman of the Year by Seagram's panel of nine assistant coaches, the award's most overwhelming winner at the time. Most significantly, he has played all his team's games in five seasons, always with braces on both knees. "If the scars could be erased, I wouldn't even feel they'd been operated on," Munoz says.

Munoz did everything he could to prove his knees were back to normal before the draft. He recovered in time to play in the Rose Bowl, where he made key blocks in the decisive late drive of USC's 17–16 victory over Ohio State. On strength tests for his quadriceps, the thigh muscles that stabilize the knee, he hit the top of the charts for both legs. He brought his 40 time back down to normal, a whisker under five seconds. "He's a rare specimen," Gregg said. "He moves better than any big man I've ever seen."

"He's awesome physically," Robinson said, "but basically he's a good all-around athlete with speed." He just happens to be bigger than most good all-around athletes with speed. He wasn't much slower in college than Charles White, Southern Cal's Heisman Trophy tailback. On a 34-yard screen pass, Munoz ran step for step with White and made the last block for his touchdown. For the Bengals last year, he caught a short touchdown pass on a tackle-eligible play in the fourth quarter, tying a game Cincinnati won in overtime.

Munoz attributes his quickness to the baseball and basketball he played in high school, growing up near Los Angeles in Ontario, California. "I weighed 270, and so there was always the challenge of guarding a guy quicker than me," he says. "And in baseball, I played third base. That's guaranteed to improve your lateral quickness."

He started playing baseball when he was 6 or 7. His childhood dream was to sign a major league contract and buy his mother a house. It wasn't a pipedream either. He was scouted heavily as a high school pitcher before he developed shoulder trouble in his senior year. He took his football scholarship at USC because the Trojans would let him play baseball, too.

"Baseball was my first love," he says. "Football to me in high school was something to keep me in shape for baseball. I never felt I was that good at it. When I was young, I was always too big for my age group in Pop Warner football, so they never let me play."

As a sophomore, Munoz pitched in relief for Southern Cal's 1978 national champions. His record was 1–0 with 13 strikeouts in 11 innings. He would have been in the starting rotation the next year, but football injuries ended his baseball career.

His only full season was his sophomore year.

"He's awesome physically," said Rams coach John Robinson, "but basically, he's a good all-around athlete with speed." He just happens to be bigger than most good all-around athletes with speed.

He tore right knee ligaments as a freshman and again as a junior. Ten plays into the first game of his senior year, his first game after the second operation, he tore left knee ligaments. He made it his goal to come back for the Rose Bowl. "Each time I was hurt, I felt bad because I couldn't play in the Rose Bowl," Munoz said. "The last time I knew I had the time to come back. I knew it would take about three months to rehabilitate my leg." The day he came home from the hospital, Munoz was skipping rope on his good leg. He started lifting weights with the bad one before the cast came off.

Munoz's rookie year was also Gregg's first with the Bengals. Gregg had called him the foundation for rebuilding an offense that had ranked 23rd in NFL yardage the year before. The Bengals had allowed 63 sacks, most in the league. "I look at it as a challenge, not pressure, " Munoz said. "It gives me incentive to improve."

By the end of his first season, Riverfront Stadium was scattered with Munoz banners—for an offensive lineman! He made all the all-rookie teams. But while others talked about his becoming the best offensive lineman of all time, Munoz talked about all the things he had to improve. One of his goals for the next season, he said, was to make the team.

"I'm super-critical of myself," Munoz said after his rookie season. "I've got to watch that. I know I made a lot of mistakes, but instead of just trying to work on these things, I kind of get down on myself."

The Bengals went 6–10 in Munoz's rookie year, but they were 12–4 and AFC champions in 1981, then 8–1 in 1982. Both those years, they ranked second in total yardage and third in passing yardage. By 1981, their sacks had dropped to 35, 12th in the league.

Quickness is what usually sets great offensive linemen apart. Strength they can build in the weight room. Munoz always has been quick, of course, but it was his strength that set teammates abuzz. He was overpowering. His first few days in training camp, he was knocking veteran defensive linemen on their behinds.

Unlike most offensive linemen, Munoz came into pro ball more advanced at pass blocking than at run blocker. His lateral speed was one reason, but so was his college, which had two other blockers in the top 11 draft choices for 1980 and 1981. "We worked on both aspects of the game," Munoz said. "A lot of schools, all they do is run, run, run." Munoz had the strength for run blocking, but the techniques there favor more aggressive behavior. "That's something I have to work on," he said. "You have to have that meanness on the football field. You've got to go out there and take that upper hand. The only way you can quiet someone down is to physically quiet them down."

Playing against Munoz has become a sobering experience, but not necessarily a silencing one. In fact, his opponents often can't say enough about him. As Lee Roy Selmon, Tampa Bay's all-pro defensive end, put it, "He's the best young offensive lineman I've ever played against."

OZZIE NEWSOME
HE NEVER STOPS SHINING

Cleveland Browns
Born March 15, 1956, at Muscle Shoals, Alabama
Height, 6.02. Weight, 232.

			PASS RECEIVING			
YEAR	**CLUB**	**G**	**NO**	**YDS**	**AVG**	**TD**
1978	Cleveland NFL	16	38	589	15.5	2
1979	Cleveland NFL	16	55	781	14.2	9
1980	Cleveland NFL	16	51	594	11.6	3
1981	Cleveland NFL	16	69	1002	14.5	6
1982	Cleveland NFL	8	49	633	12.9	3
1983	Cleveland NFL	16	89	970	10.9	6
1984	Cleveland NFL	16	89	1001	11.2	5

Fireworks attract more attention than street lights. That's why Ozzie Newsome didn't start in a Pro Bowl until his seventh NFL season. Someone was always more dazzling at tight end, usually Kellen Winslow. But no one has been more consistent. No one has been easier to take for granted.

There is no higher compliment in a game where coaches fear nothing more than the unexpected. Newsome's problem is that fans tend to associate reliability with insurance companies, not football heroes.

When Newsome is the pass receiver, "It's like throwing to an octopus who can run," says his Cleveland Browns quarterback, Paul McDonald. "I know he's not going to drop it. Even if it's a real tight fit, he'll find a way to get it."

Newsome has never missed a start in his 105-game pro career. He has caught passes in 103 of them, including the last 82. In 1983 and again in 1984, he had 89 catches, tied for seventh most in NFL history. He is 40 catches shy of the league record for tight ends, Jacki Smith's 480. And in the six seasons both Winslow and he have played, Newsome is the NFL's leading receiver, with 402 catches to Winslow's 399.

His teams haven't been so good. Only the 1980 Browns went to the playoffs. But that shouldn't

**"It's like throwing to an octopus who can run,"
says Newsome's quarterback, Paul McDonald.**

detract from what Newsome has done. It makes
him all the more valuable. Often, he has been his
team's only beacon of hope.

Imagine the numbers he might have with a
good team. Newsome's 89-catch seasons were
against defenses designed specifically to stop
him. Who else were they going to worry about?
The 1983 Browns didn't have another receiver
with more than 37 catches, and the runner-up last
year had 35. The 1984 Browns had the NFL's
24th-ranked quarterback and placed 18th in passing yardage. "It's very obvious that if you want to
begin to stop our offense, you've got to stop Ozzie
Newsome," Sam Rutigliano said when he
coached the Browns in 1983.

"I want to be the best tight end in the league,"
Newsome says. "I can't do everything great, but I
do everything well enough to put me up there
with the best tight ends in the game."

The Browns have given him enough different
things to do. He was their deep threat in his first
few seasons, after they selected him 23rd in the
1978 draft. He averaged as many as 15.5 yards
per catch, more than a lot of wide receivers. More
important, he stretched out the defenses. People
said he didn't block like a tight end. He was
always racing off downfield. But he took defenders with him, and that opened up room for both
the running game and short, high-percentage
passes.

"Every time you get some speed that teams
have to respect, that takes something away from
them," said Brian Sipe, Newsome's first Browns
quarterback. "When we got the speed to stretch
those deep zones, the game made a lot more
sense to me."

In Newsome's fourth season, 1981, the Browns
decided they had to get him the ball more often.
"He's so good the coaches create plays for him,"
Sipe said. On plays where he had been blocking,
now he was drifting out as a safety-valve receiver. His receptions increased from 51 to 69.

Since then, he has evolved to more of a tradi-
tional tight end, specializing in short catches over
the middle, keeping drives alive on third-and-
eight. But to make it harder for opponents to
double-team him, the Browns have lined Newsome up everywhere from the backfield to the
sideline. "It seems the more the coaches expect
from him, the better his concentration," Sipe said
before going to the USFL in 1984.

"No one in the league goes after the ball better
than Ozzie," Rutigliano said. "He does all the
things Kellen Winslow does, and there isn't a
receiver in football who catches the ball in traffic
the way he does. He gets some hellacious shots
and he doesn't get separated from the ball. He
gets up and plays hurt."

Newsome's reliability may have led ironically to
one of the most painful recent memories in
Browns history. In their 1980 playoff game, the
Browns trailed the Raiders 14–12 but were driving in the last minute. Sipe threw a pass toward
Newsome at the back of the end zone. It never
dawned on him that Newsome might not find a
way to catch it. But on the icy field, Newsome
couldn't cut back in front of safety Mike Davis,
who intercepted the pass. The game was lost.

Newsome made big touchdown catches in two
fourth-quarter rallies that season, when the
Browns were 11–5. But the Pro Bowl recognition
came one season late, as it often does. The 1981
season was Newsome's only Pro Bowl year until
1984. It also was the year the Browns rejoined
NFL also-rans with a crashing fall to 5–11.

"Not winning has been very frustrating," says
Newsome. "I'd take going to the Super Bowl over
the season I had. I'd give up 50 or 60 catches for
five or six more wins. Records are made to be
broken, but people remember winners."

They honor them, too. Newsome has seen that
from both sides of the won-lost column. "When I
was at Alabama," he says, "I didn't catch a lot of
balls, but I made all the All-America teams simply
because we won."

There may have been other reasons. Alabama coach Bear Bryant called Newsome "the best end I ever coached, because not only was he a great receiver, but he had exceptional concentration, fine speed and great hands." He played wide receiver then, and his career average of 20.3 yards on 102 catches was a Southeastern Conference record. As a senior, he was the conference's Offensive Player of the Year.

In high school, Newsome was all-America in both football and basketball. But playing for Bryant was as far-fetched as running for President throughout most of his boyhood in Muscle Shoals, Alabama, a town of 2,000 in the state's northwest corner. Separate eating sections in the backs of restaurants were a way of life. Newsome went to high school with the fresh memory of Governor George Wallace literally blocking blacks' admission to the University of Alabama. The school's trustees didn't really start re-examining their racial policy until 1972, when Alabama got whomped by Southern Cal and its explosive black running back, Sam Cunningham.

"During my lifetime, that's when it all started to change," Newsome says. "My folks were proud I could go to the same school as the kids of the people my parents worked for."

He still goes back to Alabama every spring. He helps the Crimson Tide coaches with spring practice. Newsome admits to being an unreconstructed country kid. During football seasons, he misses the South's friendliness. Besides, he has another dream. Ten years ago, he might not have been able to mention it even inside his family without seeing everyone's eyes roll.

"Not winning has been very frustrating," says Newsome. "I'd take going to the Super Bowl over the season I had. I'd give up 50 or 60 catches for five or six more wins. Records are made to be broken, but people remember winners."

He wants to be a major college's head coach. "The day I stop playing football, I'd like to be able to step into coaching without a lapse," he says, "and I use the off-season to prepare me for it." Some would say he has made good use of the on-season, too.

WALTER PAYTON
NOBODY DOES IT BETTER

Chicago Bears
Born July 25, 1954, at Columbia, Mississippi
Height, 5.10. Weight, 202.

YEAR	CLUB	G	RUSHING ATT	YDS	AVG	TD	PASS RECEIVING NO	YDS	AVG	TD
1975	Chicago NFL	13	196	679	3.5	7	33	213	6.5	0
1976	Chicago NFL	14	311	1390	4.5	13	15	149	14.9	0
1977	Chicago NFL	14	339	1852	5.5	14	27	269	10.0	2
1978	Chicago NFL	16	333	1395	4.2	11	50	480	9.6	0
1979	Chicago NFL	16	369	1610	4.4	14	31	313	10.1	2
1980	Chicago NFL	16	317	1460	4.6	6	46	367	8.0	1
1981	Chicago NFL	16	339	1222	3.6	6	41	379	9.2	2
1982	Chicago NFL	9	148	596	4.0	1	32	311	9.7	0
1983	Chicago NFL	16	314	1421	4.5	6	53	607	11.5	2
1984	Chicago NFL	16	381	1684	4.4	11	45	368	8.2	0

PASSING ATT	COMP	PCT	GAIN	TD	INT	AVG
1	0	00.0	0	0	1	0.00
-	-	-	-	-	-	-
-	-	-	-	-	-	-
-	-	-	-	-	-	-
1	1	100.0	54	1	0	54.00
3	0	00.0	0	0	0	0.00
2	0	00.0	0	0	0	0.00
3	1	33.3	39	1	0	13.00
6	3	50.0	95	3	2	15.83
8	3	37.5	47	2	1	5.88

Walter Payton plays football. That's such an obvious thing to say, but the point got lost last year, in the stampede of media coverage that followed him past Jim Brown's rushing record and through his first playoff victory in 10 seasons with the Chicago Bears.

The voracious appetite of media maxi-coverage isn't satisfied by simply playing football. It hungers for personalities, not performers. It prefers Dick Butkus as Bubba Smith's straight man to Butkus as the standard for middle linebackers. But Payton doesn't do talk shows, and he does very few commercials. He plays football.

He plays the game as well as anyone has played it, maybe better. Bear coach Mike Ditka said he always thought Payton could have been the greatest triple-threat quarterback. He even used him at quarterback for six plays. "Walter's the whole package," Ditka says. "He may not do some things as well as someone else has done, but he does everything better than anyone else ever has."

His legacy is as a complete player. It was ironic that he entered the national spotlight only when the country noticed he was about to run for more yards than any running back in history. Calling Payton a great runner is missing the field for the hash marks. He blocks like no other back, often lifting blitzers and defensive linemen off their feet. He kicks 60-yard punts and field goals in practice. He has thrown seven NFL touchdown passes and led the league in kickoff returning. And Bear fullback Matt Suhey says, "The strongest part of his game is his pass receiving."

Payton's blocking is what separates him from other great ground gainers. It also links him with football's working class. He says it's how he shows his appreciation to his teammates. "He doesn't want to be one of the untouchables, where guys can't talk to him," Suhey says.

But Payton has to block well for another reason. He has to prove he can do it, if only to himself. "Walter has a tremendous ego on the football field," Suhey says. It's an ego that takes pride in the game's drudgeries, not a false vanity in putting himself above them. "He doesn't want to look bad. He's a guy who hates to be told, 'You did terribly.' So he takes the same pride in blocking or receiving that he does in running."

Even growing up in Columbia, Mississippi, Payton didn't play football until 11th grade because he couldn't bear to be second fiddle to his older brother, Eddie. He left Jackson State with 464 points, an NCAA record that still stands, but wondered why he had been overlooked in the Heisman voting. The scouts didn't miss him. He was the first running back and fourth player drafted in 1975. In the Bears' first rookie camp, he insisted on going last in all the physical tests so he could break the records in each one.

In his early seasons, he was a practice-field sideshow. He caught punts behind his back. He threw passes 70 yards. He leapfrogged a 6'5" assistant coach who was standing erect. He walked 50 yards on his hands. He threw footballs at other balls as they sailed over the goalpost, hitting one of every three.

But he was serious about football. Even in his 10th season, teammate Dan Hampton said, "Walter still plays like he's trying to be the best tailback in the 10th grade." He still follows a workout regimen so grueling, he says it takes an hour to complete it and a day to recover from it. He doesn't have to work like an undrafted rookie desperate to make the team. But he must.

"If you don't, whatever you accomplish, you'll

Even in Payton's 10th season, Dan Hampton said, "Walter still plays like he's trying to be the best tailback in the 10th grade." He still follows a workout regimen so grueling, he says it takes an hour to complete it and a day to recover.

look back and say, 'Damn. If I did that, and I only worked so much, just think what I could have accomplished if I'd exerted myself to the fullest.' Why put yourself in that position? Just go ahead and do it."

He wants to be remembered, he says, "like Charlie Hustle, Pete Rose. I want people to say, 'Wherever he was, he was always giving his all.' " Teammates will remember him for, as Gary Fencik says, "his intensity and his personality." Historians will record his achievements.

To Payton, Brown's 12,312-yard record was barely a resting place, much less a stopping place. "I'm shooting for 15,000 or 15,500," he said. "I want to break the record by so much, everyone else will break their hearts trying to catch it. Jim Brown's record just happens to fall in my path. I set my sights for goals that are beyond my reach, so if I do fall short of them, I've accomplished even more than I thought of."

That hasn't been easy. Before the Steelers cut Franco Harris last summer, Payton thought it was outrageous enough to set the goal of beating Harris to Brown, gaining 687 before Harris gained 362. And now that he's 997 beyond Brown, 15,500 is just two 1,100-yard seasons, 267 below his full-season average.

"Most athletes compare themselves with other athletes," teammate Mike Singletary says. "But if Walter did that, he'd be limiting himself. He has to set standards based on the best he thinks he can do, which is more than the others have even thought about doing."

So records become stepping stones, not pinnacles. Payton likes the chase better than the finish. "Records are like dreams," he says. "Good while you're having them, but when you wake up, you can't remember what you were dreaming about."

Payton passed Brown in the sixth game last year, taking a pitchout around left end for six yards. It was not an otherwise memorable play, but it is hard to pick out memorable plays from a career that has reduced the spectacular to commonplace. He doesn't even have a trademark, aside from maybe his scissors-legged stride. He's too versatile. He can dance and make tacklers grab for air on one play, then lower his head and make them gasp for air on the next. Power and speed are the primary ingredients in the package, but he still pulls away from cornerbacks on long touchdown runs.

The way to learn about Payton is to watch him, not to listen. He accommodated the media show last year. His answers were funny, thoughtful, revealing, insightful, touching, and diplomatic—

better than ever in his career. It was as if someone had told him snappy interviews were another part of being a complete player. But he was true to himself. "I'm not like one of those game birds who shows his feathers to attract a mate," he says. "I'm not flamboyant." Whenever he could, he deflected the spotlight to the teammates who were helping win the division and end the nine-year frustration of 61–70. He was sincere about preferring the victory to the record on the day he passed Brown.

He went into the season with one memorable record, his 275-yard game in 1977, the year he was the league's MVP. He finished with not only the rushing record, but also records for 63 100-yard games, eight 1,000-yard seasons, 3,047 carries, 17,511 combined yards, and three 2,000-yard seasons from scrimmage. He has had three of the NFL's top 11 rushing seasons. Perhaps his most impressive record is unofficial, 142 consecutive games, missing only one as a rookie. In a sport where each carry can end a career, Payton's longevity only enhances his record.

"There'll never be another Walter Payton," Ditka says. "When it's all said and done, Walter may be remembered as the greatest, period."

Payton wants to be remembered, he says, "like Charlie Hustle, Pete Rose. I want people to say, 'Wherever he was, he was always giving his all.' "

MIKE QUICK
IT ALL ADDS UP TO THE SCOREBOARD

Philadelphia Eagles
Born May 14, 1959, at Hamlet, North Carolina
Height, 6.02. Weight, 190.

			PASS RECEIVING			
YEAR	CLUB	G	NO	YDS	AVG	TD
1982	Philadelphia NFL	9	10	156	15.6	1
1983	Philadelphia NFL	16	69	1409	20.4	13
1984	Philadelphia NFL	16	61	1052	17.2	9

The only thing Mike Quick sheds more freely than defensive backs is labels. He's not quick, for one thing. Headline writers have tried to have fun with his seemingly ideal name for a wide receiver, but "quick" doesn't fit this Quick.

He doesn't seem fast, either, when you see the 4.6 written next to his 40 time, but Quick's long strides shred that nugget of information to dust. Try telling the cornerbacks he leaves behind that Quick isn't fast. For that matter, try telling them he's graceful. He *looks* graceful. His running style is as fluid as, well, quicksilver. Watching that, it's hard to believe he's such a strong, tenacious blocker. Defensive backs believe it, though. They probably aren't even surprised to find out this low-key gentleman has an offbeat collection of more than 50 hats and owns three Arabian show horses and their Southern California ranch.

Quick's opponents have learned to look past his first impressions. Open the door to this Chevy and you can climb into a Cadillac.

Quick won't fit in any pigeonholes. As his teammate, Philadelphia Eagle quarterback, Ron Jaworski, says, "He's a guy you can count on for popping a deep one and breaking a game open, but he's also a guy you look for over the middle on third-and-six." There may be better game-breakers, and there may be better possession receivers, but none of them share the same body.

Sports connoisseurs put nearly as much stock in labels as wine buffs, so Quick's mercurial image has left him underrated most of his career. That's OK, he says. "I like to be the underdog. Let the doubting Thomases keep doubting me. That's my advantage." If he blew his cover by showing up in the last two Pro Bowls, that's fine, too. To

Quick, double coverage is just one more obstacle to bring to its knees.

The thing Quick does best is gain yards. Now there's something everyone can agree on. He led all NFL receivers with 1,409 in 1983, the highest league total in 16 years. He was down to 1,052 in 1984, still 12th in the league. His 22 touchdowns for those two seasons trailed only St. Louis' Roy Green and Seattle's Steve Largent, whose teams each scored nearly twice as many touchdowns as the Eagles.

"Mike can take any kind of pass and go all the way with it," Eagle coach Marion Campbell says. "The thing that continually amazes me about him is what he does after he makes the catch. He can shake defenders by juking them or by taking them straight on. People tend to forget that he's very strong."

What Quick shows after the catch is the same combination of speed and tenacity that makes him so hard to categorize. It's a hard quality to measure, but the Eagles thought they might have been drafting it because they scouted Quick as a whole player, and it added up to more than his parts. "We had a highlight film of him and most of it was blocking," personnel director Lynn Stiles said. "I liked his toughness and ability to go into a crowd."

Blocking was Quick's main job at North Carolina State. He set the school's all-time receiving record, but it was like a record snowfall in Jamaica. He played for a running team.

When the Eagles looked ahead to the 20th choice in the 1982 draft, the wide receiver they wanted was Perry Tuttle, who had 4.4 speed and 52 catches for Clemson's national champions. But Buffalo traded for the 19th pick and swiped away Tuttle. The Eagles had to settle for Quick, the fourth wide receiver in the draft. They had no idea the first three would warm their benches for three seasons. Tuttle was cut twice.

"You try to make the most educated decisions you possible can," Stiles said. "You study films and you send out scouts and you pore over evaluation reports. Then, after you do all that, you have to get lucky sometimes."

Being a consolation prize didn't insult Quick, it challenged him. "I guess you could say everything worked out for the best," he said later. "I always knew what I could do. I knew that, given the opportunity, I could play with anybody."

Opportunities never came easily for Quick. He

"This is the best time in all of football history to be a wide receiver," Quick says. "You can do so many things you couldn't do a few years ago."

grew up in public housing in Hamlet, North Carolina, a railroad town of less than 5,000 people. His mother worked as a domestic and nurse's aid to feed 10 children. Quick would get up at 5:30 to take a bus to the fields, where he picked tobacco, cucumbers, and peaches. He would collect garbage for the Job Corps. "If things come too easy, you don't appreciate them," he says now. "I learned to work for things."

He played hard, too. His Richmond High School track and football teams won state championships. His best sports were basketball and track, where he eventually ran the 110-meter hurdles in 13.8 seconds, nearly world class. He didn't settle on football until after high school, when he spent a year at Fork Union Military Academy in Virginia, hoisting his grades and learning discipline.

Football still was a struggle for Quick in his rookie year, when the NFL strike made everything tough for rookies and he made just 10 catches. But the next year, his teammates voted him the Eagles' MVP when he gained 31 percent of their yardage and scored 13 of their 27 touchdowns. "There isn't anybody in this league who can cover Mike alone," Jaworski said.

Quick gained 100 yards six times in 1983, including four in a row. Nine of his 69 catches went at least 40 yards, and his 20.4-yard average was the league's second best. Obviously, he was faster than he looked. "I run with the same motion at full speed as I do when I'm just starting," he explained. Other Eagles started calling him Silk.

"He's so smooth you don't realize how fast he's going," Eagle cornerback Herman Edwards says. "Those long strides can lull you to sleep. You don't realize how much ground he is covering, and all of a sudden, he's in your face and it's too late. His speed is deceptive. He's sneaky fast."

Speed is overrated, Quick says. He's a wide receiver, not a sprinter. "You can run a 4.2 forty, but if you can't run a good route and know how to get open it doesn't matter. You've got to run under control. Fred Biletnikoff ran a 4.8, but he knew how to get open and catch the ball."

Harold Carmichael was in his 13th season when Quick was in his second, but Carmichael said he learned a lot about playing wide receiver from his younger teammate. The kid caught the ball with his hands. He didn't wait for it, and maybe give someone time to tip it. He reached for it.

"He's a competitor," Jaworski said. "He's a fine downfield blocker. That indicates to me a guy who wants to play. It's not just 'Throw me the ball,' He'll do whatever you ask of him."

Just put that opportunity within reach, and get out of the way. "This is the best time in all of football history to be a wide receiver," Quick says. "You can do so many things you couldn't do a few years ago. In that sense, I feel fortunate. I've come along at the right time for my position. I plan on taking advantage of it."

"There isn't anybody in this league who can cover Mike alone," said Eagles quarterback Ron Jaworski. Other Eagles just call him "Silk."

GERALD RIGGS
FINALLY, THE ONE BACK

Atlanta Falcons
Born November 6, 1960, at Tullos, Louisiana
Height, 6.01. Weight, 230.

YEAR	CLUB	G	RUSHING				PASS RECEIVING			
			ATT	YDS	AVG	TD	NO	YDS	AVG	TD
1982	Atlanta Falcons NFL	9	78	299	3.8	5	23	185	8.0	0
1983	Atlanta Falcons NFL	14	100	437	4.4	8	17	149	8.8	0
1984	Atlanta Falcons NFL	15	353	1486	4.2	13	42	277	6.6	0

YEAR	CLUB	G	KICKOFF RETURNS			
			NO	YDS	AVG	TD.
1982	Atlanta Falcons NFL	9	-	-	-	-
1983	Atlanta Falcons NFL	14	17	330	19.4	0

For a month, people had wondered if the Atlanta Falcons' running game would spend the 1984 season on the shelf, tucked away like an outgrown sweater. William Andrews, their best runner the previous five years, was lost for the season and perhaps forever. His injured knee looked like it had been through a food processor, with shredded ligaments and even nerve damage. Now the burden would fall on a quiet, young fullback who still had enough baby fat for coach Dan Henning to call him Cheeks.

The rest of the football world knew him as Gerald Riggs, the promising 1982 rookie who did not start a game in his first two NFL seasons. How good was he really? Well, he seemed pretty good when he played, but he hadn't played all that much. Certainly not enough to tell. When Riggs made his first start in the 1984 opener, he was still a prospect.

Three hours later, he was a budding star. He carried the ball 35 times for 202 yards. He led Atlanta to a 36–28 upset over New Orleans. He earned the starting job that he had inherited.

"Making Gerald a starter was like holding a red flag up to a bull," Falcon placekicker Mick Luckhurst had said when Andrews was injured. "Gerald is getting that green light, and you know how much Gerald has been waiting for that chance."

By the end of the season, Riggs ranked fourth in the NFL with 1,486 rushing yards, fifth with 1,763 yards from scrimmage, and tied for third with 13 rushing touchdowns. Although he missed a game and a half with an ankle injury, Riggs finished just 81 yards short of the team rushing record Andrews had set the year before.

"I don't know if I'm deserving of a record," Riggs said late in the season, "but I think I'm deserving of a little more respect, maybe from people outside our team."

Riggs had been the ninth player and second running back in the 1982 draft, right ahead of Marcus Allen, and it wouldn't have surprised anyone if he had been the fourth or fifth pick. "We really didn't feel like we could pass him up," Falcon general manager Tom Braatz said. But Riggs had been lost in a star running back's shadow before he landed under Andrews. He had gone from Bonanza High School in Las Vegas, where he was the only boy in a seven-child family, to Arizona State, where he played in the Pacific Ten Conference at the same time Allen was setting rushing records for Southern Cal. Riggs ran for 891 yards as a senior, nearly 1,500 fewer than Allen, and it escaped most fans' attention that he was a gifted inside runner who also led the Pac-10 with a 6.0-yard average.

The Falcons were going to pair him with Andrews in the NFL's most powerful backfield. Even though he didn't start as a rookie, he ran more often for more yards than the halfback ahead of him, Lynn Cain. He was all set to start the next year, but then the Falcons changed coaches and Henning installed the new one-back offense.

Henning's tactic made more sense than his critics admitted. The same offense had helped win a Super Bowl for Washington, which had both John Riggins and Joe Washington worthy of starting. Riggs would play. He wouldn't start, but if the one-back improved the team's running game, there would be more carries for everybody. Riggs and Andrews couldn't have the ball at the same time anyway. With only the ball-carrying back in the game, the other one could rest on the bench instead of taking a beating as a blocker.

There was one problem. Logic didn't feed Riggs's hunger for action. He just wanted to play. Never mind that he hadn't been much of a blocker in college. He had called blocking "something I realize I need to improve and am willing to develop." Good players want to be good at everything, and it only frustrates them to protect them from their weaknesses with substitutions.

"The most difficult thing was trying to figure out what my role was going to be," Riggs said.

When the Falcons' star back William Andrews was injured in 1984, he told Riggs, "Don't try to fill my shoes. You've got your own shoes to fill."

The depth chart didn't have a name for someone who shared the running load in a one-back offense and ran more than many two-back teams' fullbacks but didn't start. To Riggs, all that still spelled back-up. He carried 100 times in 1983, leading the team with eight touchdown runs. He decided he was just going to have to beat out Andrews, if that's what it took to make him a starter.

"I didn't come into this season looking at it as another year of playing back-up," Andrews said, looking back to the 1984 training camp. "When camp started, it was going to be an all-out thing. William loves to play, but so do I. I was there to challenge him for the starting job, and I was really coming on strong."

He was clearly bigger and faster than Andrews, with the breakaway acceleration to run for a 40-

When the Falcons' star back William Andrews was injured in 1984, he told Riggs, "Don't try to fill my shoes. You've got your own shoes to fill."

yard touchdown against San Francisco in 1983. Bill McPherson, the 49ers' defensive line coach, had compared him with Riggins, the Redskins' bull of a runner who had the speed to outrun Miami's defense for Washington's winning Super Bowl touchdown. But Andrews was one of the NFL's best, the only running back to make all four Pro Bowls in 1980–83. For the three nonstrike years in that stretch, Andrews never had fewer than 1,300 yards rushing or 50 catches. He was a consummate blocker and receiver, and Ram coach John Robinson said he "might have been the best second-effort runner in the league." Veteran linebacker Jack Reynolds calls him, "the one player who gives the tackler more punishment than the runner gets."

None of which mattered when Andrews wound up in the hospital. "Don't try to fill my shoes," Andrews told Riggs. "You've got your own shoes to fill."

Henning's only concern had been for Riggs's durability. He never had carried more than 15 times in a game. He didn't know what it was like to come from the huddle, ears still ringing from being tackled four plays in a row, and take the ball once more into a defense that knew he was coming. He had never been through the blow-by-blow test of averaging 24 carries a game, getting hit from three or four directions each time. As Riggs admitted late in the season, "I never really had a view of what it really takes to play every week and to take all those hits the whole game."

The ankle injury may have slowed him down. Before it, he had a five-week total of 619 yards, two behind the NFL leader. He had three of his five 120-yard games in those early weeks, when his average gain was 5.0 yards. It was only 3.8 after Riggs returned to the lineup. But when the Falcons were losing nine straight games and the offensive line was falling apart, he kept coming back for more. He set a team record with 353 carries. Looking ahead to Andrews's possible recovery, he said, "I'm not the kind of guy who likes to lose something once I get it."

To the Falcons who knew Riggs, his season wasn't a surprise. It only proved what they had suspected all along. Andrews had barely been carried from the field when quarterback Steve Bartkowski said, "I've always thought Gerald might be the second best running back in this league. But he hasn't had the chance to light up and do it."

LEE ROY SELMON
THE SOLID FOUNDATION

Tampa Bay Buccaneers
Born October 20, 1954, at Eufaula, Oklahoma
Height, 6.04. Weight, 263.

YEAR	CLUB	G	SACKS
1976	Tampa Bay NFL	8	5
1977	Tampa Bay NFL	14	13
1978	Tampa Bay NFL	14	11
1979	Tampa Bay NFL	16	11
1980	Tampa Bay NFL	16	9
1981	Tampa Bay NFL	14	6½
1982	Tampa Bay NFL	9	4
1983	Tampa Bay NFL	14	11
1984	Tampa Bay NFL	16	8

Lee Roy Selmon wouldn't hurt a mosquito unless it tried to move the ball against Tampa Bay. He's a model citizen, the Boy Scout manual come to life. Modest and dedicated, courteous and good natured. It's a good thing, too, "If he wasn't nice, they'd have to bar him from football," says Abe Gibron, the 10th-year veteran's only pro defensive line coach before this season.

For a defensive end voted Pro Bowl starter the last six years, Selmon has earned unusual admiration from the men he battles. Not the awe that grows from fear. The kind of respect that made Chicago tackle Ted Albrecht wish he had gotten to know Selmon personally. "He has a sense of etiquette on the field," Albrecht said. "He has ethics."

"He could go inside you or around you, but when he beat you, he didn't try to embarrass you with it," recalled Stan Walters, Philadelphia's former Pro Bowl tackle. "He just got ready for the next play."

Selmon takes competition to its highest level, where its purpose is for great athletes to bring out the best in each other. He takes his position a step or two past the clouds, too. His 78½ sacks in nine years is misleadingly low because he has been double- and triple-teamed so often. It says more that 1984 was the fourth year Selmon forced at least four fumbles. But the best tribute to Selmon, still widely considered football's best pass-rushing defensive end, is that Tampa Bay had one of the last 3–4 defenses to use four linemen on passing downs. The Bucs could afford to leave an extra man in pass coverage because as a pass rusher, Chicago defensive coordinator Buddy Ryan says, "Lee Roy counts for two."

"If it were just a matter of putting him up against a single blocker, it would be no contest," Gibron says. "He's one of the greatest defensive ends to ever play this game. You very seldom have to raise your voice to Lee Roy because he seldom makes a mistake."

Even when Selmon was young, Detroit coach Monte Clark said, "Watching him is like watching a grown man at work among a bunch of boys." Albrecht was a rookie in 1977, one year after Selmon, and he recalled how he felt at halftime of his first Bucs game: "I told the coach my deepest secrets. I said I never wanted to be buried at sea, I never wanted to get hit in the mouth with a hockey puck, and I didn't want to go out and play that second half against Lee Roy."

The NFL Players Association has named Selmon Defensive Lineman of the Year in 1979, 1980, 1982, and 1983. In 1981, he was co-MVP of the Pro Bowl with four sacks. "He could win all the awards possible," says Gibron, "and all his teammates would still appreciate him. Because he never gloats on his ability. In fact he's a little shy on it."

To Selmon, he is nothing special. Just one of nine children from a tight farm family in Eufala, Oklahoma. His parents were special. They made ends meet in hard times. "Two of the greatest parents God ever put on earth," Selmon calls them. "We were taught to respect, to behave, and to do our best. All nine kids turned out pretty good. I'm not better than any of the rest."

As an adult, Selmon's family remains his proudest honor. He unabashedly prefers the company of his wife, Claybra, and three children to the fast track at any pro athlete's beck and call. His charity work helped make him one of the U.S. Jaycees' 1982 choices for America's 10 Outstanding Young Men.

At first, young Lee Roy wanted to be an auto mechanic. It looked more interesting than slopping hogs and milking cows. Football was not an instant attraction. He nearly quit after one practice with the junior high team, but his mother persuaded him to keep trying.

Lee Roy was her last child. She had delivered three of them within 3½ years, Lucious II and

Often weighing in the low 240s, Selmon looks small by defensive ends' standards. But his arms could paddle a river boat. Or, as former Bucs coach John McKay put it, "Whenever I want to feel good, I think about Lee Roy Selmon."

then Dewey, who was 11 months older than Lee Roy but in the same school class. "They were my examples really," Lee Roy says. "I patterned myself after them. I tried to keep up with them." School desegregation came in time for only the last three Selmons to play football. Lee Roy and Dewey would be teammates for 15 years, from eighth grade on to the Bucs, until Dewey was traded to San Diego after the 1981 season.

The family splurged for a black-and-white TV when Lee Roy was in first grade, shortly after the farm got electricity. Soon came the rule that it stayed off on weeknights. The set had distracted Lucious, and he flunked fifth grade. When he brought the news home, his father gave him the reins to the plow mule and said, "That's what you're going to be doing the rest of your life." It was the last time, through college, any of the three brothers got a grade lower than B.

As a senior at Eufala High, Lee Roy played tailback and averaged 14 yards per carry. He wanted to play quarterback, but even his 70-yard touchdown pass in practice didn't change the coach's mind. He was all-state in basketball, but there was never any doubt that he and Dewey would join Lucious on Oklahoma's football team. The Sooners went 43–2–1 in Lee Roy's four-year career. As a senior, he led the 1975 national champions with 132 tackles, despite opponents' tendency not to test his side of the field. He won the Outland and Lombardi awards as college football's best lineman. He became the first choice in the 1976 NFL draft, the first draft choice ever for the expansion team from Tampa.

That team lost its first 26 games in two seasons. "It was tough to live with," said Selmon, who would patronize the McDonald's drive-in window to avoid facing people in restaurants. The Bucs improved to 5–11 in 1978, but after 14 games, Selmon needed surgery for torn knee ligaments. When his cast came off five weeks later, a week ahead of schedule, he went straight to the weight training room. He wanted the knee strong enough to forget about it and play instinctively in 1979.

Selmon's 1979 season wouldn't fit on just one highlight film. He had 11 sacks, 60 quarterback pressures, and 117 tackles, leading a defense designed to have linemen close the gaps and linebackers make the tackles. The Bucs went 10–6, won their division, and played for the NFC championship in their fourth season. When Selmon was named the NFL's Outstanding Defensive Player, he said the award was meant for the whole defense, which yielded league lows of 246.8 yards and 14.8 points a game. "I can't say it's a dream come true," Selmon said, "because I never dared to dream of such a thing."

By defensive ends' standards, Selmon looks small. He often weighs in the low 240s. But his arms could paddle a riverboat. Besides criterion speed and strength, his success stems from exceptional balance and tireless determination. "He's always chasing people," Gibron says. "I've seen him bust through two guys and run down a quarterback." He's the sort of player that makes linebacker Hugh Green, a young all-pro himself, call it "an honor and privilege to play on the same side as Lee Roy."

Or, as nine-year Bucs coach John McKay put it: "Whenever I want to feel good, I think about Lee Roy Selmon."

Chicago Bear tackle Ted Albrecht once told his coach, "I never want to be buried at sea, I never want to get hit in the mouth with a hockey puck, and I don't want to go out and play that second half against Lee Roy."

BILLY SIMS
A WONDER TO WATCH

Detroit Lions
Born September 18, 1955, at St. Louis, Missouri
Height, 6.03. Weight, 225

YEAR	CLUB	G	RUSHING				PASS RECEIVING			
			ATT	YDS	AVG	TD	NO	YDS	AVG	TD
1980	Detroit Lions NFL	16	313	1303	4.2	13	51	621	12.2	3
1981	Detroit Lions NFL	14	296	1437	4.9	13	28	451	16.1	2
1982	Detroit Lions NFL	9	172	639	3.7	4	34	342	10.1	0
1983	Detroit Lions NFL	13	220	1040	4.7	7	42	419	10.0	0
1984	Detroit Lions NFL	8	130	687	5.5	5	31	239	7.7	0

The sideline can be a hectic place. Defensive players have to hustle to the Gatorade in case their teammates can't make a first down. They might need a quick confab over that blocking scheme that gave them fits on the last series. It's nice to sit down for a moment, too. They don't always see every play.

But if Billy Sims has the ball, necks start craning. "He's incredible," Detroit defensive tackle Doug English says. "When he starts to zoom and gets 6 yards, then 8 yards, and when they start hitting him, he starts falling forward and sliding under them for extra yards. And about that time, they'll start going lower and he'll jump over all of them for about 30."

Sims doesn't look as though he's up to doing all that. He stands an inch shorter than his listed 6 feet. He doesn't seem to weigh 212, either. Where other backs have tree trunk legs, Sims has fence posts. His 4.45 time in the 40 isn't slow, but he's not one of the fastest running backs. Just one of the most electrifying. As Sims puts it, "I know how to stir excitement."

The first time he ran from scrimmage in a Lions uniform, Sims started routinely toward the practice field's right sideline, turned upfield and accelerated. He didn't stop until he had a 65-yard touchdown. Quarterback Gary Danielson looked at coach Monte Clark and noticed goose pimples on his arms.

Five years later, Sims holds every Lion rushing record worth reaching for. He has been running better and farther than other backs ever since he started in Little Hooks, Texas, where he gained

7,738 yards and scored 516 points in high school. In college, Sims set NCAA records with average gains of 7.1 yards for his career and 7.6 as a junior, when he was the sixth underclassman to win the Heisman Trophy. In the NFL, he went to Pro Bowls his first three seasons, and although injuries interrupted the last two, his per-game averages are 85.1 yards rushing and 34.5 on pass plays.

He always seems to be a big play about to happen. "With great backs you can see vibrations going," Clark said when he was coaching Sims, "and you can feel you're going to do it right then and there."

Vibrations explain Sims's success as well as anything. His physical assets don't begin to do it, but then, Sims considers physical tools overrated for a back who wants to do more than just run and fall down. Some of the best singers don't have very good voices either, but they capture ears the way Sims captivates eyes.

Sims calls intelligence a running back's most important asset. "Speed without wisdom will get you caught every time," he says. Much of that intelligence has to be instinctive. A back has to anticipate, to see things before they're there.

"A good running back knows how to make sharp, fast cuts," Sims says. "But the ability to make them isn't as important as the instinct to make them at the right time. Things happen so fast in football that you have to react to them without thinking."

Courage is another of Sims's intangibles. Maxie Baughan, Detroit's defensive coordinator in Sims's early years, said Sims reminded him of Gale Sayers, whom he called "the hardest back to intimidate" when he was playing. "He's a relentless player," 49er coach Bill Walsh says. "We probably have more respect for him than any other ball carrier, and maybe any other player."

And beyond all that, former Lion backfield coach Bill Johnson said, "For a guy who's in the superstar status, Billy's just a super team player. He does the grubby things that a football player has to do." He not only plays hurt, he practices hurt. He blocks. He's a willing decoy. He defends teammates on the field and laughs with them in the locker room. They respect his work habits and like his personality. "A good running back is always looking to make a contribution," he says. "Football games aren't won by one or two people. They're won by a committee."

Sims was the man of the house when he was little, the oldest of five orphaned children living with his grandmother in East Texas. He helped support the family by pumping gas, hauling hay,

The first time Sims ran from scrimmage in a Lions uniform, he didn't stop until he had a 65-yard touchdown. Quarterback Gary Danielson looked at coach Monte Clark and noticed goose bumps on his arms.

chopping cotton, even working on stadium clean-up crew after games. He was inspired by his mentally retarded brother to get his degree in recreational therapy. The two were so close, when Sims's brother drowned shortly before his first pro training camp, Sims said, "I'd rather it had been me than him."

Oklahoma wanted him badly enough to have an assistant coach live in a Texarkana hotel much of his senior year. His career there stuttered off to a slow start, with injuries ending both his sophomore and red-shirt season. But as a junior, he led the country with 1,762 yards rushing and fell short of 100 only when he was replaced after one quarter of a 66–7 victory. His senior year wasn't quite so spectacular, but he still was all-America. Scouts liked him enough to leave no doubt he would be the first player drafted. "There will never be another player like him at Oklahoma," Sooner coach Barry Switzer said.

With all that build-up, Sims did more than live up to expectations as an NFL rookie. The Lions' record improved from 2–14 to 9–7. They went from 25th to 3d in rushing offense, 26th to 7th in total yards. Sims's 16 touchdowns led the league, and he led the NFC in rushing until he wilted to only 113 yards in the last three games.

He gained 40 more than that in his first game alone, when he also turned a 10-yard pass into a 60-yard touchdown. The next week, he ran for 134 yards and scored from 87 yards on a short pass that he caught below his knees without breaking stride. This from a man who had caught all of two passes in college. "I felt chills every time he touched the ball," veteran linebacker Charlie Weaver said.

When Sims filled out the Lions' standard questionnaire for rookies, his answer for "Biggest thrill in football" was "Able to remain healthy my last two years." That's still a luxury. His only full NFL season was his first one. A foot injury cost him two games in 1981, when his per-game average of 102.6 yards rushing would have yielded the NFL's 11th best season. In 1982, his training camp holdout dovetailed into the strike. He had 190 yards eight games into 1983, when the Lions were 3–5 and Sims had missed all but one series of four games with a broken hand. In the last eight games, he ran for 850 yards and the Lions went 6–2, winning their first divisional championship in 26 years.

Last year, Sims's best start ended with his worst injury. Clark blamed his torn knee ligaments and cartilage on Minnesota's artificial turf, which he said was "like a cheap house rug." Despite playing only eight games, his 687 yards rushing led the Lions, whose 4–11–1 record was the worst in Sims's career. Once again, the burden falls to Sims to lead his team up the ladder.

"I like the competition," he says. "That's what I like about any game, seeing how well I can do against the other guys. I don't like to lose, but if I haven't done my best, winning isn't much fun, either. The competition is what appeals to me."

MIKE SINGLETARY
A COMPLETE PLAYER

Chicago Bears
Born October 9, 1958, at Houston Texas
Height, 5.11. Weight, 230.

YEAR	CLUB	G	SACKS
1981	Chicago NFL	16	0
1982	Chicago NFL	9	1
1983	Chicago NFL	16	3½
1984	Chicago NFL	16	3½

It was a slap in the face. When the Chicago Bears' nickel defense took the field on passing downs, Mike Singletary was banished to the bench. Plays were going on and Singletary was missing them, leaving the dinner table after the salad. And the embarrassment was even worse. It didn't matter that hardly any NFL middle linebackers played in nickel defenses. The stadium announcer might as well have said, "Mike Singletary is coming out of the game now because there are some things he can't do."

"My goal has always been to be a complete player," Singletary says. "To do whatever I can the best I can, better than anyone else. When you take a guy out, that says, 'You can't do this.' You can put icing on it, but the bottom line is, it's saying you're not a complete player."

That wouldn't do. Singletary told his team-mates before his third season, 1983, he'd be on that nickel before the season ended. "He was begging me," defensive coordinator Buddy Ryan says. More than that, he was making himself "as good a pass-defense linebacker as there is in the league," Ryan says now, after Singletary has played every down for the last year and a half.

"He *willed* himself onto the nickel defense," Fencik said. "We kidded him about it. Three guys had to get hurt before he got in, but once he got in, no one was going to get him out."

It was another goal, and Singletary topples goals like he topples running backs. His other 1983 goal was to make the Pro Bowl, which he did the last two years. For 1984, he set his sights on Defensive Player of the Year. He made it, for the NFC, as the Bears led the league in practically every defensive category.

Even as a rookie, Singletary looked like a hatching legend. More precisely, he played like a legend. "I haven't seen a linebacker play with his intensity since I played with Dick Butkus," defensive tackle Jim Osborne said. He even made the same popping sound when his pads hit ball carriers.

That's what fans want in middle linebackers. It's nice that Singletary is an anachronism, a middle linebacker who plays on third-and-eight, but fans are more quick to notice he's a throwback who makes the earth move. They don't swap fond stories about Butkus's interceptions. They remember his hits.

They remember some of Singletary's, too. In his second start as a rookie, he hit Kansas City halfback Joe Delaney so hard, safety Doug Plank said, "It sounded like a vacuum cleaner. You could hear the air being sucked out of Delaney's rib cage."

"Whenever Mike makes a big stick, he has a big smile in the huddle," cornerback Terry Schmidt said. "He can't wait to come out again for more." Even if he's the stickee, Singletary says he's thinking "Just bring it again. I feel if a guy hit me that hard, it's going to be a fight. I want to make sure he gets some of it, too."

He doesn't want to leave scars. If he knocks a player out of the game, he needs to visit the locker room or call him to find out he's OK to play next week. Singletary isn't a mauler, he's an artist, painting with his shoulder pads.

"When you get a good hit, it lasts all game," he says. "It's rare that you get the opportunity. You can't get the guy from the side. You may knock the crap out of him, but you'll hurt yourself, too. When you hit a guy straight-on, with good form, the helmet right where it should be, the right lift, that's thrilling. That's excitement."

In college, Singletary broke nine of his helmets.

"I haven't seen a linebacker play with his intensity since I played with Dick Butkus," defensive tackle Jim Osborne said of Singletary.

The pros could afford more durable ones, but he still impressed his new teammates with the excited noises he made as he banged heads on the practice field. They called him the Tasmanian Devil, then revised it to Samurai. Even as a rookie, he led by resounding example. "He makes an impact," Fencik says. Coach Mike Ditka was nearly as frustrated as Singletary that his missile went into its silo on passing downs. "You take him off the field, and his teammates notice his absence," Ditka said.

Singletary led by demeanor, too. Even if he didn't wear glasses, he would have the studious look of a man who was born after adolescence. Surely he never did childish things like read nursery rhymes or giggle at cartoons. In 1983, he complained that other players didn't watch films on their day off.

His youth, in a tough Houston neighborhood, was the sort that ages quickly. Two older brothers died in accidents. His parents divorced. He had pneumonia three times before he was 6. The youngest of 10 children, he says, "Even some of my sisters were taller than me." He would ask his mother why he couldn't be taller. She would tell him to take advantage of the things he had. He paid attention.

"Every year, I wanted to go out and prove things to people. I wanted to show people I can do this. I *will* do this. I'd look at that guy who's 6'3" and 240 pounds and say, 'I can do that better than he can.' It's not size, it's desire. I think my lack of size gave me the drive to prove it, show it, do it."

At Baylor, Singletary was the Southwest Conference Player of the Year his last two seasons. He averaged 15 tackles a game, with never less than 10 and three games in the 30s. The only goals he didn't reach were winning the Heisman Trophy and growing to 6 feet. His lack of height enabled the Bears to draft him in the second round. "I think our computer blew a bulb on that one," Cowboy coach Tom Landry later said of the oversight.

Singletary's biggest problem was that he had rarely seen a pass except on the turnpike. Who passes in the SWC? "I came to camp weighing 240," he says. "At that weight, not knowing what to do, I looked like a clown. I didn't even know how to read linemen so I could tell if it was going to be a pass or a run. Goodness. We could be playing San Diego, and I'd be playing the run."

So the next off-season, he dropped his weight to 225 and studied film of defensive backs covering receivers. He had the speed. His 100-yard time in high school was 9.8. The next season, he kept

"Whenever Mike makes a big stick, he has a big smile in the huddle," cornerback Terry Schmidt said. "He can't wait to come out again for more."

Bear receivers on the field after practice. He wanted to keep up with wideouts. He talked to the defensive backs, the coaches. What could he do to improve?

It's not enough to be the best pass-defense *linebacker*. That's almost like being the best tackler of all NFL placekickers. "I think I drive Buddy crazy," he says. "Every time he turns around, I'm asking him, 'How far am I?' How far am I from being the best linebacker ever? It's the only way to be."

Ryan answers bluntly. More interceptions, he says. And anyone can be more consistent. "He wants criticism," teammate Todd Bell says. "He doesn't like it. But he does something about it." Even if Singletary is watching film from two months ago, it infuriates him to see himself make a mistake. "I'll keep playing that film back until I figure out what I should have done to make the play," he says.

He has so much more to do. "I want to be like Dick Butkus against the run and Willie Brown against the pass," Singletary says. "I'm not going to stop until I get there."

JAN STENERUD
THE KICKS JUST KEEP ON COMING

Minnesota Vikings
Born November 26, 1943, at Fetsund, Norway.
Height, 6.02. Weight, 190.

Year	Club	G	XP	XPM	FG	FGA	Pts
			PLACE KICKING				
1967	Kansas City AFL	14	45	0	21	36	108
1968	Kansas City AFL	14	39	1	30	40	129
1969	Kansas City AFL	14	38	0	27	35	119
1970	Kansas City NFL	14	26	0	30	42	116
1971	Kansas City NFL	14	32	0	26	44	110
1972	Kansas City NFL	14	32	0	21	36	95
1973	Kansas City NFL	14	21	2	24	38	93
1974	Kansas City NFL	14	24	2	17	24	75
1975	Kansas City NFL	14	30	1	22	32	96
1976	Kansas City NFL	14	27	6	21	38	90
1977	Kansas City NFL	14	27	1	8	18	51
1978	Kansas City NFL	16	25	1	20	30	85
1979	Kansas City NFL	16	28	1	12	23	64
1980	Green Bay NFL	4	3	0	3	5	12
1981	Green Bay NFL	16	35	1	22	24	101
1982	Green Bay NFL	9	25	2	13	18	64
1983	Green Bay NFL	16	52	0	21	26	115
1984	Minnesota NFL	16	30	1	20	23	90

When Jan Stenerud kicked a 54-yard field goal last season, Viking teammate Randy Holloway told him, "That's one you can tell your grandchildren about." Then Holloway clarified himself. "Today," he added.

You want age gags? Fine. Stenerud can do age gags. "It must have barely made it because I couldn't see it," he said. "My eyes aren't that good anymore."

If it's field goals you want, Stenerud's your man

there, too. Fifty-four yards was the longest in the NFC last season. The week after that one, Stenerud kicked five field goals in the Vikings' 29–28 victory over Detroit. He kicked them in spite of losing his regular holder during the week. A few weeks later, his 53-yard field goal with two seconds left beat Tampa Bay 27–24. Those three games were the only ones Minnesota won.

At 42, Stenerud had lots of people rubbing their eyes in disbelief. He made his first Pro Bowl in eight years, connecting on 20 of 23 field goal attempts. He didn't miss from 46 yards on in. Even from 50 on out, he was 3 for 4, the most he had ever made from that far.

"I thought he was too old to have that much leg left," Tampa Bay rookie Keith Browner said. "I thought you get worse with age instead of better."

That's what the Kansas City Chiefs had thought four years earlier. They cut Stenerud in their 1980 training camp. Since then, his field goal percentage has been .823. In 1981, Stenerud made 22 of 24 field goal tries for Green Bay. His .917 percentage broke a 28-year-old NFL record.

But the Packers gave in to age prejudice after the 1983 season. They carried two placekickers that year. Eddie Garcia kicked off. He seemed to have a bright future on field goals, too. Stenerud had to go.

Packer coach Forrest Gregg later called it his worst move of the year. Garcia had to be replaced by midseason, and Stenerud cost the Vikings just a seventh-round draft choice. So what if he was nearly four years older than coach Les Steckel? The Vikings cut two returning veterans to make room for Stenerud, then replaced the stool in front of his locker with a rocking chair.

Steckel had met Stenerud four or five years earlier. They had decided to play tennis. "Jan and I grabbed two rackets and ran five miles to the courts," Steckel said. "We played an hour and a half and ran back five miles."

So Steckel wasn't surprised when Stenerud arrived barely in time to warm up for his dreaded obstacle-course run and nearly won the darn thing. He had the best time among kickers and quarterbacks, and he hadn't even practiced on the course, like the other Vikings. "The last few years, when I realized each year could be my last, I've been running more," Stenerud said.

He always had been a good athlete. He's one of the NFL's best golfers. But his first love was ski jumping. Stenerud grew up in Festund, Norway, outside Oslo, and was his country's sixth-ranked ski jumper at 18. The next year, he went to the

Viking players celebrated Stenerud's 42nd birthday with a cake that said, "Happy 52nd Birthday." They gave him a four-legged walker.

University of Montana on a skiing scholarship.

"The original plan was to go one year," Stenerud says. "Just to see another part of the world for the adventure of it." But the ski jumpers liked to run up and down the steps of the football stadium for their workouts. Sometimes, they would watch the football team practice. One day, some football players were kicking extra points after practice. They invited the foreign kid down to join them.

Stenerud lined up straight behind the ball. That was the only way he had seen a football kicked. But he was wearing tennis shoes. There had to be an easier style on his toes. He had seen soccer players line up at an angle for penalty kicks. They hit the ball with their insteps.

That worked. Stenerud kept backing up until he was splitting the uprights from 50 yards. When football coach Jim Sweeney asked him to try kicking off, Stenerud kicked the ball through the goal post 70 yards away. Sweeney looked into his visa status.

Stenerud couldn't play that season, but Sweeney had him on the sideline for the last home game. He wanted him to get used to big crowds. "He didn't realize that I had ski jumped before 70,000 people in Norway," Stenerud says.

The best season Stenerud had for the Chiefs was his third, in 1969, when he made 27 of 35 field goals, a .771 percentage he has topped in three of the last four years. He also made 16 in a row in 1969, an NFL record that lasted 10 years. He helped the Chiefs win the Super Bowl with a 48-yard field goal, and the next year he kicked another 48-yarder in the Pro Bowl—both are still records.

"It's a very insecure job, but you don't get beat up," Stenerud has said. "To stay around, you can't have too many bad days. I always felt if I had two bad games in a row I'd be out. That's the kind of pressure I put myself under."

The Chiefs decided he was over the hill after 1979, when Stenerud was 12 for 23 with three blocked field goal attempts. They replaced him with Nick Lowery, now the NFL record-holder in career field goal percentage. Stenerud went into business with a partner designing a tee for soccer-style kickers. He didn't join the Packers until his 38th birthday, in November 1980. They decided to keep him after his 53-yard field goal in a 1981 exhibition game.

"I think the question about my range has always been raised by people who put my age in front of my name," Stenerud said. "I may not have the range I had 13 or 14 years ago, but my leg's as good as the average kicker in the NFL." Since then, Stenerud has been 20 for 32 from 40-plus yards and 5 for 7 from 50 or more, far ahead of his Kansas City stats of 73 for 176 and 12 for 52.

The Chiefs actually gave him a year when their press book mistakenly listed his birthday as 1943 instead of 1942 in the mid-seventies. "Don't tell them," punter Jerrel Wilson advised. "You'll get old soon enough." He said he didn't let the Packers know when he turned 40, "because that might have been reason enough for them to cut me."

Now he can scoff at the calendar. Viking players celebrated his 42nd birthday with a cake that said "Happy 52nd Birthday." They gave him a four-legged walker. Stenerud has made age an

"It's a very insecure job, but you don't get beat up," Stenerud has said.

advantage, learning with experience how to scout a sloppy or windy field before the game, how to stick to good mechanics and take his time under all conditions.

"The important thing is to be consistent all season," he says. "It isn't always that easy. You've got to be in the groove for four or five months."

His one concession to age is the special brace on his left ankle. "Most of the wear and tear has been on my left ankle, planting it over and over again," Stenerud says. It hurt bad enough in the 1984 training camp that he nearly retired before trainer Fred Zamberletti supplied the brace.

He finished the season with the NFL's all-time record for field goals, but he trailed George Blanda's scoring record by 389 points. That was a good four seasons away. Even if he can play that long, Stenerud is unlikely to have grandchildren. His oldest child will only be 19.

DWIGHT STEPHENSON
CENTER OF ATTENTION

Miami Dolphins
Born November 20, 1957, at Murfreesboro, North Carolina
Height, 6.02. Weight, 255.

YEAR	CLUB	G
1980	Miami Dolphins	16
1981	Miami Dolphins	16
1982	Miami Dolphins	9
1983	Miami Dolphins	16
1984	Miami Dolphins	16

There they go again, calling Dwight Stephenson the greatest center in the game. He should be used to it by now. When he played at Alabama, no less an expert than Bear Bryant called him the best center he had ever seen, let along coached. But that kind of talk makes Stephenson shudder. What good is being an offensive lineman if people are going to keep pointing you out? Stephenson may live the glamorous life of a pro football player, but he takes to the limelight like a duck takes to gravel.

It's nice to be respected and all, but the way Stephenson sees it, compliments are the first step to complacency. Which, of course, is right at the devil's elbow. He knows football isn't anything more than whipping the guy across from him play after play after play. And nobody ever whipped the guy across from him with press clippings.

So when that nonsense kept coming up while he prepared for the Miami Dolphins' Super Bowl game last January, Stephenson said, "I know I'm not the best center in the league at this time." He won't even admit to being the best center in his class at Alabama. "I think I have some good games. I also have some bad games. Maybe people only see the good games."

What they see is a combination of strength and quickness that may be unprecedented among NFL centers. In fact, it probably wouldn't have been wasted on a center 10 years ago. The conventional wisdom used to be that centers didn't have to be draft choices, let alone high ones. Jim Langer, Miami's great center in the 1970s, was a free agent. He may not have been the greatest athlete in the world, but there wasn't anyone more tirelessly determined and competitive. That's what teams wanted in their centers.

But the game is different now. Langer rarely lined up helmet-to-helmet with a defensive tackle, as Stephenson does against the predominant 3–4 defenses. Centers have to be strong now, as well as dogged. So instead of moving him to guard, the Dolphins have let Stephenson set the standard for centers in the 1980s. He's got the blue-collar ethic of the old-time centers *and* the body of a battleship. When he was named Seagram's Offensive Lineman of the Year in 1983, he was the first center ever to win the award.

Stephenson's strength enables the Dolphins to pair him off with the nose tackle and concentrate on the rest of the line's matchups. Nearly every offense has to double-team nose tackles. It's just not a fair fight for the center. The nose tackle can pounce as soon as the center's hand moves, but the center still has his hand between his legs. Stephenson, though, is not only strong enough to handle the nose tackle, he makes a habit of driving his man so far off the line, he picks off a linebacker, too.

His quickness is even more impressive. That's important against either a nose tackle or a middle linebacker in a 4–3 defense. One of Stephenson's first plays that switched on the national limelight was against San Diego's 4–3 in 1982. He fired out on middle linebacker Cliff Thrift so quickly, the block was made practically before the quarterback had the ball. With Thrift out of the way, the ball carrier gained eight yards up the middle. Of course, the way Stephenson saw it was, "We were both going the same way," never mind that Thrift was going backward.

Stephenson's quickness is one reason the Dolphins allowed the fewest sacks in the NFL in both 1983 and 1984, 23 one year and 14 the next. To put that 14 in perspective, the next best team was sacked 27 times. Stephenson can snap the ball and set up so quickly, it's like having an extra lineman. He can either handle one man by himself or scamper over to help a teammate with, say, the opponent's best pass rushing defensive end or linebacker.

"He's a complete center in every sense of the word," Miami coach Don Shula says. "He's strong, he's quick, and he's a tremendous competitor. He goes all out on every play. He's the guy who makes it all work on our offensive line."

Stephenson's first Pro Bowl trip was after the 1982 season, when he was an alternate. By 1983, it

"When he says he isn't playing well, he's still playing better than most centers," says Fred Smerlas, one of the league's best nose tackles. "He's the best center in the league."

was vogue to call him the best center in football, surpassing Mike Webster, Pittsburgh's perennial all-pro Goliath. Stephenson started in that year's Pro Bowl and made most all-pro teams. He was one of only three offensive players to start for the Dolphins' offense in both Super Bowls after the 1982 and 1984 seasons. The awards accelerated in 1984, when he won all three awards given for Offensive Lineman of the Year.

Stephenson wasn't buying any of it. "By no means am I having as good a year as I had last year," he said. "I'd be happy if I could play just one game through without making any major mistakes. I just want to cut down on my mental errors. There are times when I'll take a man on short when I should be dropping back and letting him come to me. I'll get a little bit overaggressive."

For one thing, Stephenson had a harder go of it last season because the word got around that he was the toughest brick to crack on Miami's front wall. For another, "When he says he isn't playing well, he's still playing better than most centers," says Buffalo's Fred Smerlas, one of the NFL's best nose tackles. "He's the best center in the league."

It just isn't his nature to be flashy. If he has to be in headlines, he'd rather get there for ending a crime spree, as Stephenson and teammate-neighbor Don McNeal did when they helped police catch three men responsible for more than 30 home burglaries. Otherwise, he'd rather not have any ink beyond his roster listing.

"He's been like that ever since I've known him," says McNeal, who was a college teammate. "At Alabama, when they were saying all this stuff about him being the greatest center that ever played there, he was always saying, 'Nah, not me. They did it, they did it.' "

Stephenson has the ideal personality to play offensive line, football's most thankless and demanding spot. He had a brief trial at defensive end for Alabama, but he says, "After three days, they put me back. I like offense a lot better than defense."

He played center at Hampton (Virginia) High School. He's a center, period. He was the third center drafted when the Dolphins took him on the second round in 1979. He didn't crack the starting lineup until the 12th game in 1981, when he replaced injured Mark Dennard.

It has never come as easy for Stephenson as he makes it look. He hopes he'll never let it. Often, he grades himself lower than the coaching staff does. He may be a rising star, but that's largely because he remains a shrinking violet.

"I don't want to get to the point where I think I'm good," Stephenson says. "When you get to that point, you get overconfident. Then I'll make more mistakes than I already do. My goal every week is to play a complete game. I want to keep working and getting better every week."

LAWRENCE TAYLOR
AN AMERICAN ORIGINAL

New York Giants
Born February 4, 1959, at Williamsburg, Virginia
Height, 6.03. Weight, 237.

YEAR	CLUB	G	INTERCEPTIONS				SACKS
			NO	YDS	AVG	TD	
1981	N.Y. Giants NFL	16	1	1	1.0	0	10.5
1982	N.Y. Giants NFL	9	1	97	97.0	1	7.5
1983	N.Y. Giants NFL	16	2	10	5.0	0	9
1984	N.Y. Giants NFL	16	1	1	1.0	0	11.5

For some reason, people talk about originals as if they are cookie cutters. Lawrence Taylor was not the first blitzing right linebacker in a 3–4 defense, but he defined the position in just one season. Ever since he burst into—and through—the NFL in 1981, coaches have been begging scouts to find them "another Lawrence Taylor," as if it were as easy as shopping for Calvin Kleins. They haven't found one. There is no other Lawrence Taylor, of course.

He is 6'3", weighs 243 pounds, and runs like a halfback. "The fastest linebacker I've ever seen," says Sam Huff, the ex-Giant linebacker in the Hall of Fame. Taylor can rush the passer, turn around after the ball is thrown, and catch the receiver downfield. He holds a team record with a 97-yard touchdown on an interception return. And strong? Taylor tosses 270-pound offensive linemen aside the way others rummage through a closet.

He was the inspiration for Washington coach Joe Gibbs's one-back offense. "Putting another tight end on the line of scrimmage was the only way to block Lawrence Taylor," Gibbs said. At first, opponents tried to use running backs to block Taylor. That didn't work. They barely slowed him down. San Francisco found a solution in the 1981 playoff game against Taylor, assigning guard John Ayers to track him down. Ayers kept Taylor off the quarterback, but it was a one-game solution. It left the middle wide open for other blitzers. The job was clearly going to take more than one man. A tight end, say, and a running back, and an all points bulletin for the linemen to look for Taylor if they're not needed elsewhere.

That's what Tampa Bay tried last season. "Our

whole game plan was devised to take care of him," said quarterback Steve DeBerg. Still, Taylor had four sacks in a 17–14 victory. "He creates total chaos," DeBerg added.

Taylor was the first rookie ever to be named Most Valuable Defensive Player. He won the award the next year, too, before slipping to runner-up in 1983. For four seasons, he has been all-NFL and a Pro Bowl starter.

He didn't start playing football until he was a junior at Lafayette High School in historic Williamsburg, Virginia, where he grew up in a middle-class family. Baseball and basketball were his sports. He still plays basketball with the Harlem Wizards. But he grew 4 inches and 20 pounds before his senior year, and went on to star as a defensive end at North Carolina. As a senior, Taylor was Atlantic Coast Conference Player of the Year and made 16 quarterback sacks.

The numbers on North Carolina's light blue uniforms were hard to see when Giants general manager George Young scouted Taylor. Soon, though, it didn't matter. "Every time there was a big play, Lawrence Taylor made it," Young said.

The Giants made him the second pick in the NFL draft. They disappointed fans who had hoped for a running back. "We need an impact player," the fans said. That was in the pre-Taylor NFL. Now it's almost a cliché to talk about "impact players on defense."

He forced six fumbles last season, an almost unheard-of figure, and two more in the playoffs. He has had 38½ sacks in four years, never less than his 7½ in the nine-game 1982 season.

"A sack is like a touchdown for the defense," Taylor says. "Any time you get a sack, it turns the momentum toward the defense and forces the offense to try to hit the big play."

The only question Young had about Taylor as a rookie was "how soon we were going to be able to line him up as a first-team linebacker." Ability wasn't the issue. "We knew he had the ability," Young says. "But you can't put a rookie in right away. The veterans will resent it."

So the Giants had to wait a few days. After the first scrimmage, when Taylor had four sacks and a fumble recovery, the players would have resented keeping him *out* of the lineup. In his first exhibition game, Taylor had ten solo tackles, two sacks, and a fumble recovery. Quarterback Phill Simms couldn't wait for the season to start so he wouldn't have to play against Taylor anymore.

The rookie had no awe. When Taylor knew he was blitzing, he even was brazen enough to wink at the quarterback. So what if the other team

Ever since Taylor burst into the NFL in 1981, coaches have been begging scouts to find them "another Lawrence Taylor," as if it were as easy as shopping for Calvin Kleins. They haven't found one, of course. There is no other Lawrence Taylor.

knew? "They've still got to stop me," he said.

"When Lawrence Taylor is pass rushing," said Beasley Reece, then the Giants' free safety, "it's like a cop putting sirens on top of his car. Lawrence puts a light on his helmet. His hands are flopping and his arms are swinging. He attacks and destroys the blocker, and then he goes after the quarterback or the ball carrier."

Taylor was the main difference in the Giants' improvement from 4–12 in 1980 to 9–7 and their first playoff berth since 1963. When they won four of their last five games, they did it without scoring more than 20 points. They didn't give up more than 10.

"The great thing about Lawrence Taylor is he plays in such bad humor every Sunday," Young said. But that's not entirely true. Taylor plays the game for the game's sake, not for a love of mayhem.

"There's nothing better than a real good, solid

tackle," Taylor says. "I love to hit and get hit. If a quarterback holds the ball too long, I'm going to let him know. I've put a couple people out in my day, but I don't want anybody to get hurt. I always pray before a game that nobody gets hurt. It's OK to stun them, but I don't want any broken bones."

When Taylor's salary didn't keep pace with his stature through two seasons, he held out in 1983. He hated it. He couldn't keep himself from going to watch his teammates work out. He reported without a new contract, then wound up signing briefly with the USFL and costing the Giants $750,000 to buy out the contract for the privilege of making him rich.

But Taylor's 1983 memories are miserable. The Giants were 3–12–1. Taylor talked seriously about quitting. He deeply resented the teammates he felt weren't putting out. He tried to do it all himself. He moved to inside linebacker because of an injury, volunteered to play on kicking teams, and even offered to play tight end, too, an idea coach Bill Parcells rejected.

"I want to be part of a winning team," Taylor said. "I can hold my head up high knowing I've done my best, but that's nothing like hearing people say, 'Ooooo, Wow!' when you say you play for the Giants. I've heard just that reaction when someone mentions the Raiders or the Cowboys."

The Giants started getting that reaction again last year. They made the playoffs with another 9–7 record, and again they did it with defense. Doubts resurfaced that anyone could block Lawrence Taylor. Taylor scoffed.

"I'm not Superman," he said. "I don't listen to praise. It's something I don't need. I don't want to get into a situation where I think I'm that good. You can always play better."

"When Lawrence Taylor is pass rushing," said Beasley Reece, then the Giants' free safety, "it's like a cop putting sirens on top of his car. Lawrence puts a light on his helmet."

JOE THEISMANN
THE MOUTH THAT SOARS

Washington Redskins
Born September 9, 1949, at New Brunswick, New Jersey
Height, 6.00. Weight, 198.

YEAR	CLUB	G	ATT	CMP	PCT	GAIN	TD	INT	AVG	ATT	YDS	AVG	TD
					PASSING						**RUSHING**		
1971	Toronto CFL	14	278	148	53.2	2440	17	21	8.78	81	564	7.0	1
1972	Toronto CFL	6	127	77	60.6	1157	10	13	9.11	21	147	7.0	1
1973	Toronto CFL	14	274	157	57.3	2496	13	13	9.11	70	343	4.9	1
1974	Washington NFL	9	11	9	81.8	145	1	0	13.18	3	12	4.0	1
1975	Washington NFL	14	22	10	45.5	96	1	3	4.36	3	34	11.3	0
1976	Washington NFL	14	163	79	48.5	1036	8	10	6.36	17	97	5.7	1
1977	Washington NFL	14	182	84	46.2	1097	7	9	6.03	29	149	5.1	1
1978	Washington NFL	16	390	187	47.9	2593	13	18	6.65	37	177	4.8	1
1979	Washington NFL	16	395	233	59.0	2797	20	13	7.08	46	181	3.9	4
1980	Washington NFL	16	454	262	57.7	2962	17	16	6.52	29	175	6.0	3
1981	Washington NFL	16	496	293	59.1	3568	19	20	7.19	36	177	4.9	2
1982	Washington NFL	9	252	161	63.9	2033	13	9	8.07	31	150	4.8	0
1983	Washington NFL	16	459	276	60.1	3714	29	11	8.09	37	234	6.3	1
1984	Washington NFL	16	477	283	59.3	3391	24	13	7.11	62	314	5.1	1

He was always a triangular peg. He didn't fit into the square-hole stereotype of a winning quarterback—standing resolutely in the pocket, looking downfield with eyes of ice, and opening his mouth only to call signals. No, Joe Theismann didn't have the discipline for that. If he didn't trip over his scrambling feet, he would trip over his rambling mouth.

"I've had my foot in my mouth so often, I should be a leather salesman," Theismann said. But that's as far as he agreed with his critics. He would harness the enthusiasm that got him into trouble. It was powerful enough to hitch a team to and watch it roll, as the Washington Redskins did. They had the NFL's best record in the last three years, including a Super Bowl championship for 1982.

Theismann has called himself "a self-pro-claimed egotist." After he was the league's MVP in 1983, he said, "Ten years ago, Joe Theismann was the biggest name in this town. But that was only in my own mind." That was when he was the rookie who insisted he should be the Redskins' starting quarterback, which didn't set too well with the veterans. The guy was weird. He actually liked the media. He had the nerve to open Joe Theismann's restaurant in Washington before he even played. "His personality has changed from cocky and egotistical to a true team leader," says defensive tackle Dave Butz, Theismann's teammate from the bad old days.

"My mouth always has preceded my performance," Theismann says. But only because he *knew* the performance was coming right up. The first pass he threw as a Notre Dame sophomore was intercepted and returned for a touchdown. He didn't get down. He told coach Ara Parseghian, "Don't worry, we'll get it back."

"I've seen Joe throw three interceptions, literally get his teeth knocked out, and then turn around and lead his team to victory," Redskin coach Joe Gibbs says. That's the other side of his ego. Even at 35 last year, behind a deteriorating line, Chicago's league-leading pass rushers called him the hardest NFL quarterback to tackle. He keeps the ball in play.

"More than anything, his greatest skill is the knack of making something out of nothing, turning a sack into a 14-yard gain," says Jets coach Joe Walton, Theismann's former offensive coordinator. "That's just a natural talent."

"I like to take risks," Theismann says. "You can't go through life wearing only brown suits and blue shoes. Sometimes I like to wear chartreuse." He is an entertainer who says, "The football field is my stage." And he is an unrepentant youth who said in 1982, "I have a 33-year-old body, but there's a lot of 12-year-old kid running around in it."

One reason he decided to go to Notre Dame was that an newspaper that covered his South River, New Jersey, High School, ran a headline that said, "Little Joe Will Get Killed at Notre Dame." He had to take the dare. He set 23 school records, including a 526-yard game against Southern Cal in torrential rain. He finished second in voting for the 1970 Heisman Trophy, which Notre Dame's publicity office had campaigned for by changing his name's pronunciation from Theesman to Thighsman.

But he still was small and wasn't drafted until the fourth round, by Miami. When the Dolphins didn't show enough interest in signing him, Theismann went to the Toronto Argonauts and led them to the Canadian League championship game as a rookie.

After his four "agonizing" years as Washington's back-up quarterback, 1974–77, Theismann finally got his shot at age 29, when coach Jack Pardee replaced George Allen and purged the Over the Hill gang. In 1979, on a team with 14 new players, he was the NFL's second-ranked passer. He hasn't completed less than 57 percent since.

But he still hadn't reached the playoffs when Washington lost its first five games under Gibbs in 1981. His name was popping up in trade rumors. He went to Gibbs's house, and they decided to accentuate the positive, which was John Riggins running out of a one-back offense. Between that meeting and the Super Bowl loss to the Raiders 2½ years later, the Redskins won 36 of 42 games.

Theismann said he had curbed his impulsive nature, at least on the field. "I don't try to do it all myself anymore," he said. "I don't have to. Now I've got faith in my teammates. I go out there

The first pass Theismann threw as a Notre Dame sophomore was intercepted and returned for a touchdown. He didn't get down. He told coach Ara Parseghian, "Don't worry, we'll get it back."

"I've seen Joe throw three interceptions, literally get his teeth knocked out, and then turn around and lead his team to victory," said Redskin coach Joe Gibbs.

every game and ask myself, all right, who's going to make the big play next?"

Often, it was Theismann. He threw eight touchdown passes in his first four playoff games and set a Super Bowl record with eight straight completions when the Redskins beat Miami. He was the second-ranked passer in 1983, when his 29 touchdowns and 11 interceptions were remarkable for his gambling style. Against the Raiders in the regular season, he threw two touchdown passes as Washington scored 17 points in the last 7:31 to win 37–35. The '83 team set a league record with 541 points, never fewer than 23, and became the first defending champ in four years to make the playoffs, let alone repeat to the Super Bowl.

"His personality on the field was what it was off the field," teammate Art Monk said. "He took charge of things."

But then came the fall, precipitated by the Raiders' 38–9 Super Bowl victory to end the 1983 season. His 12-year marriage was collapsing. Now living the fast life, Theismann's new love was actress Cathy Lee Crosby. Personally and professionally, he decided, he had spread himself too thin. "I don't want to do that anymore," he said. "I just want to play football."

Theismann had become a walking conglomerate, with his newspaper, two restaurants, radio and television shows, movie appearances, com-

mercials, banquet speaking, and even occasional White House dinners. He needed four agents to help conduct his business. He bathed luxuriantly in the limelight.

After interviewing him for the first time, one TV reporter said, "It's like turning on a faucet." His snappy quotes ranged from philosophical to self-deprecating. Would Miami's defense rattle him into interceptions in the Super Bowl? "When there's nothing to rattle upstairs, you don't worry about it." He even took the trouble to change clothes between television interviews so it looked more like each station got something different. "I like making people happy," he said. Then, when it dawned on him that his own smile was growing weaker, he limited his 1984 media appearances to after games. "I would like to try to be myself," he said, "instead of trying to be what everybody wants and expects me to be."

His performance remained steadily strong. Offensive coordinator Jerry Rhome said, "I've seen a lot of quarterbacks, as they get older, begin to think only of the money and all that. They don't want to take any chances, so they just throw the ball away. Joe doesn't do that. Joe turns bad plays into good plays."

There would be other years, and he sure didn't *feel* old. "You can never stop dreaming," Theismann says, "because when you stop dreaming you stop living."

RANDY WHITE
FULL SPEED AHEAD

Dallas Cowboys
Born January 15, 1953, at Wilmington, Delaware
Height, 6.04. Weight, 263.

YEAR	CLUB	G	SACKS
1975	Dallas NFL	14	7
1976	Dallas NFL	14	6
1977	Dallas NFL	14	13
1978	Dallas NFL	16	16
1979	Dallas NFL	15	5
1980	Dallas NFL	16	6½
1981	Dallas NFL	16	8½
1982	Dallas NFL	9	2½
1983	Dallas NFL	16	12½
1984	Dallas NFL	16	12½

He apparently waits until Sunday night to catch his breath. No one has ever seen Randy White rest during a game. That's what other players marvel about. Sure, he's quick and strong and durable and everything else a defensive tackle should be, but much of that is a gift. Playing at one speed, down after down, that's a quest.

Tom Landry, White's coach with the Cowboys, says the only other player who could match White's intensity was Ernie Stautner, a Hall of Famer now coaching Dallas's defense. White plays the same way 20 points ahead or tied in the last 20 seconds, the same way against a rookie or an all-pro. That's why Landry says, "Randy's performances range anywhere from spectacular to spectacular."

The quintessential story about White recalls a play against Philadelphia in 1980. He rushed the quarterback on a short pass to Scott Fitzkee, a high school sprint champion. Forty-nine yards downfield, the man who dragged Fitzkee down from behind was Randy White. "He never gives up on people," says Chicago coach Mike Ditka, a longtime Dallas assistant.

White's teammates appreciate that determination more than anything. They know he could get by without it. He's the strongest man on the team. He's so quick, the Redskins have guards prepare for him by blocking wide receivers. "He's simply the greatest football player in America," ex-team-mate Charlie Waters says.

When White held out for a raise through last year's training camp, there wasn't a teammate who begrudged him his vacation or the contract he eventually got. The players all but picketed on his behalf. They wore mourning armbands. They taped "Where's Randy?" signs to their helmets.

They figured he was impossible to overpay. He hasn't missed a Pro Bowl since 1977, his first year at defensive tackle. He's been all-pro since 1978, the year he was the NFL's Defensive Player of the Year. He won various Best Defensive Lineman awards in 1978, 1981, and 1982. The list of awards is long enough to put White to sleep. All that polished hardware means so much to him, he didn't even bother to call his parents to tell them he won the 1974 Outland Trophy as college football's best lineman. "You start counting your trophies and reading about how good you are," White says, "and pretty soon somebody's going to come along and knock you on your tail."

"He goes into every game scared to death that he's going to embarrass himself," Stautner says. White agrees. He worries. "You always have to be a little on edge," he says. "You may be the best in the game, and you may even believe it, but you can't sit back and relax. You've got to be constantly working to get better."

After 1980, Landry made an offhand remark about all the strong guards in the league. By the next training camp, White had broken his own Cowboy record with a 501-pound bench press. After 1978, the first season offensive linemen were allowed to use their hands, he took up karate to discourage them.

"Randy is one of the real examples of what hard work will do," says White's college coach, Jerry Claiborne. "He went from being an average football player to one of the best by nothing but hard work."

Claiborne remembers the 210-pound fullback who went to Maryland when it was a Bottom Ten school. Only two other colleges would have had him. His high school team in Wilmington, Delaware, won five games in two years. White wasn't even all-state, and this was in Delaware, not Texas. He was a .500-hitting first baseman who might have signed with the Phillies if his father hadn't insisted on college.

After his freshman season, Claiborne told White he had a chance to be All-American and play

"Randy's performances range anywhere from the spectacular to the spectacular," said Tom Landry. "He's simply the greatest football player in America," adds ex-teammate Charlie Waters.

pro ball, but only as a defensive lineman. That sounded good to White, but at the time, he weighed 212, bench pressed 300, and ran a 4.9 forty. He went to work. They gave him the key to the weight room but made him come out for meals. As a senior, he weighed 248, benched 450, and ran a 4.6. He was a two-time all-American when the Cowboys picked him second in the 1975 draft. They still don't regret choosing him over Walter Payton.

White was going to be the next Lee Roy Jordan. "I was fascinated with making him a linebacker," Landry says. He had the speed for it. He just couldn't run backward. "It was awful," White says. "I never felt comfortable at it, not for a day."

When the Cowboys moved him to defensive tackle in 1977, White thought they were giving him one last shot to stay in the league. Hardly. The Cowboys were just desperate to get him on the field. He turned out to be the next Bob Lilly. That was when Waters coined the nickname Manster, for half man, half monster. Dallas led the league in total defense, ranked second in sacks, and won the Super Bowl, where White was co-MVP.

He never has repeated his 16 sacks of 1978. He

runs into too many pairs and trios of blockers. "What he's doing is even more impressive than a lot of sacks and tackles," Stautner says. "His presence is helping free others to make the tackles." Any offense that faces Dallas has to weaken itself across the line to make sure White is accounted for.

"One on one, he's just unbeatable," says John Dutton, Dallas's left defensive tackle. "I've seen him blow past me so fast, I didn't even know he was there. He takes the heat off everyone else."

White's intensity is surprisingly cool. He doesn't say a word. He may be the hardest hitter in the league, but that's not a goal he sets. "I just go out to play," he says.

"I've never seen him get real mad," Ditka says. "I've seen him get a little disturbed at people in practice, and he batted them around like Ping-Pong balls, but he tries not to do that. He saves it for Sunday. He doesn't have any friends on the field. He goes out there to do his job the best he can, and if you're in his way, then you've got to get out of his way."

White is just as businesslike about leaving his anger on the field. His teammates don't just admire him, they like him. Another White story they tell is about the time he adopted a puppy off the streets at training camp. He nursed it to health and smuggled it home on the team plane when camp broke.

He's a farm kid at heart. He drives a pickup truck, chews tobacco, and wears blue jeans and baseball caps with fish bait insignias. He owns a small farm in Landensburg, Pennsylvania, near Wilmington. The one trophy he displays proudly is a stuffed 10½-pound bass.

The only thing White likes better than fishing is football. He likes working out, everything about it. He could do without injuries, but pain is usually just mental, he says. He missed a game in 1979 with a broken foot, but played the rest of the

"I've never seen him get real mad," said Bear coach Mike Ditka. "I've seen him get a little disturbed at people in practice, and he batted them around like ping pong balls, but he tries not to do that. He saves it for Sunday."

season on it. "It's amazing the things you can ignore," he says.

Age is another one. White already has had a long career, but he says, "They'll probably have to run me off. I'm still trying to be the best I can be and don't feel I've reached that goal yet. Plus, it's still fun, still a game. It's still the most fun I have."

JAMES WILDER
ABOVE THE CROWD

Tampa Bay Buccaneers
Born May 12, 1958, at Sikeston, Missouri
Height, 6.03. Weight, 225.

YEAR	CLUB	G	RUSHING				PASS RECEIVING			
			ATT	YDS	AVG	TD	NO	YDS	AVG	TD
1981	Tampa Bay NFL	16	107	370	3.5	4	48	507	10.6	1
1982	Tampa Bay NFL	9	83	324	3.9	3	53	466	8.8	1
1983	Tampa Bay NFL	10	161	640	4.0	4	57	380	6.7	2
1984	Tampa Bay NFL	16	407	1544	3.8	13				

For some reason, James Wilder still has the recognition factor of a city bus. Even in Tampa, fans mistake him for Buccaneer teammate Jimmie Giles. Maybe this will help. Wilder is the one over there carrying two linebackers, a defensive end, and Tampa Bay's offense on his back. The one who's almost a sure bet to gain 100 yards. He's done it in 16 of the 20 games he has started at tailback, if you add his rushing yards and receiving yards. As you should. They're both 36 inches long.

The hot item in NFL backfields is something called the complete back, a running back who can carry the ball, catch it, and block. There aren't many. There are Walter Payton, Marcus Allen, William Andrews, and Wilder. Fast company, that. Payton and Allen draw crowds just bringing

in the mail, and even Andrews eventually made a name for himself as "Plain Ol' William." But Wilder's only crowd is the one he gets lost in.

The people who appreciate him are his teammates and the ones who have to tackle him. Listen to Lawrence Taylor, the New York Giants' mountain-moving linebacker. "He's the finest back I ever played against in my life," Taylor says. Steve Courson, the Bucs guard who spent most of his career in Pittsburgh, calls Wilder, "the most bruising runner I've been around."

Wilder's style is part of the problem. He doesn't skitter down sidelines. He's fast, but not shifty fast, not dynamic or glamorous. Fast for a big man. And strong for a fast man. "He's as strong as anybody on the team," Bucs guard Sean Farrell says. "That's what makes him different."

The comparative name that keeps popping up in discussions of Wilder is Jim Brown, who set the standard for fast-moving strength. "James can just splatter a defender," says Leeman Bennett, the Bucs' new coach. After the Packers played Tampa Bay in 1984, coach Forrest Gregg said, "There were a lot of times I thought we stopped him for a three-yard gain, and when he got up it was five or six yards."

That sounds like a fullback. Wilder looks like a fullback. He goes 6'3", 225. When he came out of Missouri in the second round of the 1981 draft, scouts listed him at fullback. So Wilder spent his first 2½ NFL seasons as an I-formation fullback, which is as good a way as any to go incognito. For all anyone knows, Jimmy Hoffa could be an I-formation fullback. The job entails clearing out lanes for an I-formation tailback, watching out for blitzers of an I-formation quarterback, and occasionally taking the ball into the crowd between the guards. He wasn't out of position, just out of the picture.

The Bucs were 0–7 in 1983, Wilder's third season, when coach John McKay decided Wilder had to carry the ball more often. McKay moved him to tailback. In his first game there, he gained 64 yards on runs and 50 on passes. The next week, against Pittsburgh, he broke the NFL record for carries with 42, gaining 126 yards. "That's a lot of carries," said Franco Harris, whose record Wilder broke, "but he seemed strong in the fourth quarter. Our guys couldn't stop him."

Wilder's 219 yards on 31 carries the next week were the most in the NFL since Payton's record 275 in 1977. The Bucs even won. But in his fourth start at tailback, Cleveland linebacker Chip Banks' helmet broke two of his ribs. "Oh, how it hurt," Wilder said. "I had never experienced pain like that." He missed the remaining five games, but the Bucs rewarded him by ignoring his scheduled $125,000 salary for 1984 and signing him for $2.2 million for four years.

He earned it. In a one-back offense, Wilder had 90.6 percent of Tampa Bay running backs' 1984 workload. He ran for 1,544 yards and 13 TDs. The Bucs' second best rusher was quarterback Steve DeBerg, with 59 yards. Wilder tied a new carries record with 43 against Green Bay and broke the record for carries in a season with 407.

He seemed to be making up for all those idle Sundays at fullback. "I don't think he gets tired," Farrell said. "I'm amazed by his ability to continually take punishment."

In Wilder's first full feature-back season, the Bucs' offense rose from last in the NFL to 10th in yardage and broke nearly all its team records.

"He's the finest back I ever played against in my life," says Lawrence Taylor of the New York Giants.

Through 20 games at tailback, Wilder averaged 101 rushing yards, 26 carries, and 41 receiving yards. His 2,229 yards from scrimmage in 1984 were 15 short of Eric Dickerson's record. He made the Pro Bowl, and *Sports Illustrated* expanded its all-pro team to 12 offensive players so it could include Wilder with Dickerson and Payton.

"I've really been waiting to get to this level," Wilder said. "I've got my mind made up now that I should be all-pro every year."

He already had been an excellent receiver. In fact, he cleared 100 yards from scrimmage in seven of his 31 starts at fullback. In 1982, when Wilder was the Bucs' Most Valuable Player, he averaged 64 rushing yards and 38 receiving yards and led NFL running backs with 53 catches. He was the second leading NFL receiver when he was injured in 1983. His 85 catches last year led running backs again, three short of the NFL record.

"You throw little flares and dump passes to

James and you can almost eliminate the defensive linemen," DeBerg says. "He can get six or seven yards, and that's an excellent running play."

"He doesn't go down unless someone gets a good shot on him" says fellow Bucs running back Scott Dierking. "He's always scrapping. I've never seen a guy who can run the ball 40 times and still look as fresh as the rest of us who have done nothing."

He's usually brightening up the locker room with his smile. "Football is not just a job to me," Wilder says. "It's fun, I can't wait to get out there."

But even before his NFL purgatory at fullback, Wilder always had to wait his turn. He was relatively small until he mushroomed to 210 pounds as a high school senior. He had to spend a season at Northwestern Oklahoma A&M Junior College before going to Missouri, where he set the school's all-time rushing record and averaged 4.8 yards a carry. He worked hard growing up in Sikeston, Missouri, barely across the Mississippi River from Kentucky, on his aunt and uncle's farm. Wilder's parents had left him there with five younger brothers and sisters after splitting up.

"He works harder than any back I've been around," says fullback Adger Armstrong, a former teammate of Earl Campbell. It's contagious. As tackle Gene Sanders says, "He makes you want to put your headgear on and hit someone. When you have a horse, you want to push it along."

To which Wilder says little beyond aw, shucks. He's not the only underappreciated Buc, he says. There's no mistaking his sincerity when he sings the familiar runner's chorus about his blockers. He even explains his gratitude. He says, "The line

Wilder's 2,229 yards from scrimmage in 1984 were only 15 short of Eric Dickerson's record.

is getting me in the secondary more, and I'm not getting hit by as many big defensive linemen. These guys are protecting me. People ask about carrying all the time, but actually it seems to be getting easier."

KELLEN WINSLOW
A CLASS BY HIMSELF?

San Diego Chargers
Born November 5, 1957, at St. Louis, Missouri
Height, 6.05. Weight, 251.

			PASS RECEIVING				
YEAR	CLUB	G	NO	YDS	AVG	TD	
1979	San Diego NFL	7	25	255	10.2	2	
1980	San Diego NFL	16	89	1290	14.5	9	
1981	San Diego NFL	16	88	1075	12.2	10	
1982	San Diego NFL	9	54	721	13.4	6	
1983	San Diego NFL	16	88	1172	13.3	8	
1984	San Diego NFL	7	55	663	12.1	2	

Kellen Winslow's place in football history was safe even before he was the star of a legendary playoff game. Before Winslow, Mike Ditka had been one of pro football's best tight ends. It was Ditka's record for receptions at tight end that Winslow broke in 1980 and 1981. So Ditka was speaking with sound credentials when he said, "If you're going to talk about Winslow, you better stop and wait a few seconds before you mention any other tight ends."

He has reshaped the position in his own image. His San Diego receivers coach, Ernie Zampese, might strain the point a smidgen when he says, "He's revolutionized the role of the tight end." The position would have evolved without him. Winslow just gave it a tangible new standard.

He came into the NFL in 1979, one year after the rules changed to make it easier for receivers, especially tight ends, to escape the line of scrimmage. The rules also would increase the emphasis on passing, so tight ends would no longer be blockers first and receivers as an afterthought. In 1981, 10 tight ends caught more passes than the Number Three receiving tight end had caught in 1971. Winslow wasn't the only one playing catch. Just the best.

"If someone wanted to construct a perfect tight end, they wouldn't have to," Rams general manager Jack Faulkner says. "They'd already have Winslow."

The Chargers sensed that when they traded to move up seven spots in the 1979 draft. They spent the 13th pick on an all-American from Missouri who had played tight end only five seasons. They had something different in mind for Winslow. Instead of always stationing him next to a tackle, they would flank him toward the sideline, sometimes as far as a wide receiver. They would send him in motion. He would even turn up in the backfield. For that variety of chores, they needed a player with a tight end's strength and a wide receiver's grace.

"I don't think of him as a tight end," says teammate Charlie Joiner, the NFL's all-time receiving leader. "He's just a great receiver." He *thinks* like a receiver, former Charger safety Pete Shaw says. He thinks about advancing the ball after his catch, "while most tight ends are looking for a place to fall down."

"One of my most satisfying feelings," says Winslow, "is to have the ball and suddenly be in the open. Then it's like pinball, bouncing along from one man to another. I love that challenge."

He couldn't verify the Chargers' wisdom as a rookie, when he broke a leg in the seventh game. But he broke Ditka's record with 88 catches in 1980 and 89 the next year. He led the league in catches both years, something no NFL tight end had done. In his five healthy seasons, he has never ranked lower than third.

And his partial seasons were even better. In 1982, the nine-game strike season, Winslow had five 100-yard games. Last year, he played only seven games, missing one for a contract holdout and the last eight after tearing up his knee. But he had 55 catches at midseason. He was six ahead of Art Monk, who went on to break the single-season record. His per-game average for the last five years would make a 93.5-catch season.

"He's probably the best athlete in the game today," quarterback Dan Fouts says. "I can't imagine anybody who could do more things than Kellen can for an offense." The offense Fouts is talking about, remember, led the league in passing yards and total yards from 1980 through 1983, the years Winslow made the Pro Bowl. In 1980, the Chargers became the first NFL team with three 1,000-yard receivers and broke records for passing yards, total yards, and first downs. Then they did all that again in 1981, the year Winslow tied a 31-year-old record with five touchdown catches in a game.

But all that trumpeting still sounded flat after the Chargers were upset in the AFC championship games for 1980 and 1981. "Even if I catch 20 passes, I can't go to the Super Bowl by myself," he said.

Winslow has been rapped as a blocker, but

In high school, Winslow was an oversized bookworm—on the chess team, no less. But the football coach finally convinced him to go out as a senior. "Let's face it," says Winslow, "people don't care how good you are at chess."

Fouts says his blocking is "the key to our whole offense." That makes sense. It's true of other teams that use a roving tight end and one back. But even Winslow's blocking remains overshadowed by his own grandeur, his toughness was never questioned after the 1981 playoff game at Miami.

Winslow set a playoff record with 13 catches for 166 yards, and the Chargers rallied to win 41–38 in overtime after blowing a 24–0 lead. He never had tried to block a field goal, but he batted down the one that would have won for Miami in regulation time. "When you think about Winslow," Dolphin coach Don Shula said, "you think Superman."

His numbers didn't begin to tell the story. It was a humid day, 79 degrees, and Winslow was a big man running in motion down after down. He lost 12 pounds. His legs kept cramping. So did his neck. He bruised his forehead. His lips needed four stitches. His right shoulder kept going numb. Three times, he had to be helped from the field, and each time he returned momentarily and made a big catch. He did all this against a defense that played him for a bumper car. Twice, his shoulder pads broke.

"One thing I have never worried about is catching the ball in traffic," Winslow says. "Maybe it's because I haven't played as much football as some other guys. I just don't hear the footsteps out there that some people talk about."

Winslow didn't play any football until he was a senior at East St. Louis High School in Illinois. He was a studious homebody from a tight family of nine in a decaying industrial town. His goal was to get an academic scholarship. If that didn't pan out, he had a good job at United Parcel Service. He could keep that and go to night school. He'd get his degree somehow.

He was an oversized bookworm—on the chess team, no less. But the football coach finally prevailed on him to go out as a senior. "Let's face it. People don't care how good you are at chess," Winslow says. "They want to know what sport you play."

Winslow's football team was undefeated until the state championship game, and he was favored to win the state track meet in the discus. But underneath his collegian's body, his mettle was junior high. Athletic pressure was new to him. He dropped two late passes in the state championship game. The big crowd rattled him at the track meet, and a career at UPS started looking good. That is one reason San Diego has a Kellen Winslow Flag Football League, emphasizing teamwork, fun, and safety in low-pressure games for children 7 through 13.

He plans to get a doctorate in counseling psychology when his football career is over. He hopes that still won't be for a while. The doctor's report after Winslow's injury last year was ominous. He said the two torn knee ligaments looked like "a couple of mop-ends." The words "career ending" came up. "Oh, no. We can't have that," Winslow said.

Around the league, even opponents felt the same way. Winslow is too great a treasure to be a relic before his time. As Zampese says, "He's the type of guy who comes along once every 10 years."

"One of my most satisfying feelings," says Winslow, "is to have the ball and suddenly be in the open. Then it's like pinball, bouncing along from one man to another. I love that challenge."

796.332 LAMB
Lamb, Kevin.
Football stars, 1985
$5.95

WITHDRAWN

CENTRAL LIBRARY OGDENSBURG

MAR 07 1986

CENTRAL LIBRARY
OGDENSBURG

NORTH COUNTRY LIBRARY SYSTEM
Watertown, New York   13601